Upgrade

Published by Grammar Factory Publishing, an imprint of MacMillan Company Limited.

Grammar Factory Publishing
MacMillan Company Limited
25 Telegram Mews, 39th Floor, Suite 3906
Toronto, Ontario, Canada
M5V 3Z1

www.grammarfactory.com

Zhang, Ella.
Upgrade: How to Outperform Your Default Self to Gain Your Superpowers / Ella Zhang.

Paperback ISBN 978-1-989737-92-7
eBook ISBN 978-1-989737-93-4

    1. SEL027000 SELF-HELP / Personal Growth / Success. 2. BUS107000 BUSINESS & ECONOMICS / Personal Success. 3. SEL000000 SELF-HELP / General.

Production Credits
Cover design by Designerbility
Interior layout design by Dania Zafar
Book production and editorial services by Grammar Factory Publishing

Grammar Factory's Carbon Neutral Publishing Commitment
Grammar Factory Publishing is proud to be neutralising the carbon footprint of all printed copies of its authors' books printed by or ordered directly through Grammar Factory or its affiliated companies through the purchase of Gold Standard-Certified International Offsets.

Disclaimer

Upgrade

HOW TO OUTPERFORM YOUR DEFAULT SELF TO GAIN YOUR SUPERPOWERS

Ella Zhang

GRAMMAR
FACTORY
— EST⁰ 2013 —

This book is dedicated to my families, my parents and my sister,
for allowing, supporting and encouraging me to grow into me!

Testimonials

'If you're looking for a deeply practical guidebook to upgrading yourself, Ella Zhang's *Upgrade* might be just what you're looking for. Providing just the right amount of context and scientific research to demonstrate the validity of the claims, this book is absolutely bursting with practical steps you can practise and implement to better understand yourself, improve your outcomes, take more control of your life, and enjoy the journey along the way.'

Col Fink, author of *Speakership* and *Tribe of Learning*

'In *Upgrade*, Ella simply presents deep knowledge, practical strategies and fascinating stories to help the reader change their internal operating system to allow for external wellbeing and high performance. It is absolutely going to help anyone who takes the time to read and understand the clear framework she provides, and I really enjoyed reading this book.'

Dr Amy Silver, speaker, facilitator, mentor and psychologist, and author of *The Loudest Guest* and *Conversations Create Growth*

'*Upgrade* is an incredibly useful handbook for leaders who are ready to be serious about their self-development, and ready to accept that there is a link between their self-care and their long-term success. It digs down into the different levels of the self with credibility and a practical orientation.'

Glenn Martin, writer, learning designer and consultant

'When I first met Ella over ten years ago, she was a curious and enthusiastic learning and development manager at an international bank based here in Sydney. Even then it was obvious she would be a coach as she was both intrigued and passionate about the human condition and understanding how best to support people to shift their results. Since those early days I've followed Ella's journey as she has transitioned from corporate executive into building a successful coaching practice with clients across the globe. I'm very excited that she has finally put pen to paper and started unfurling some of the many ideas and coaching concepts she has been developing. Ella's approach to coaching is unique and I love how she explores different perspectives in her book, especially the concept of the different "operating systems" we have. She has much more to share and I'm already looking forward to the next instalment!'

John Smallwood, thrive master coach and coach principal at the Engenesis Coach Academy

'*Upgrade* is a complete step-by-step guide to renewing your whole being and will help you reach your full potential in life and work. It is filled with anecdotes, research and quotations from thought leaders around the world. I highly recommend it.'

Alex Feher, founder and CEO, Impact Asia Pacific

'Ella has written a delightfully readable book that shares honest and real-world insights about what we all need to do to thrive in the complex and competitive world we now live in. Ella shares hard-earned personal lessons, examples from people who "upgraded" their operating systems, with simple but powerful tactics, in a direct, friendly, and at times humorous way. We need to face some harsh truths if we're to thrive because our four operating systems drive how we show up in the world. Jump into this book if you want to become a better, healthier, calmer and nicer leader – and human! It deserves to be read by everyone who is feeling overwhelmed, stressed and suffering from "infobesity"! Thank you, Ella, for sharing your unique and refreshing wisdom with us!'

Dr Delia McCabe, cognitive resilience consultant, neuroscientist, speaker, and author of *Feed Your Brain: 7 Steps to a Lighter, Brighter You!* and *Feed Your Brain: The Cookbook*

Contents

Acknowledgements

Writing a book is by far the hardest project I've ever said yes to!

None of this would have happened or been possible without the inspiration and encouragement of the faculty of Thought Leaders Business School, as well as my fellow thought leaders: Matt Church, Lisa O'Neil, Kate Billing, Col Fink ... to name just a few.

I'm eternally grateful to Ingrid Messner, the fellow leadership expert who introduced me to Thought Leaders Business School. During our decade-long friendship, she not only stood by me during all the challenges and struggles, but also inspired me to take the challenges head on. 'You can surely do this,' she often said to me, and when my self-doubt creeps in, she is the person I will call. Thank you for our weekly chat, and hikes on beaches and in the bush; I could not ask for better ways to recharge the body, mind and soul.

Immeasurable appreciation to Dr Amy Silver, who mentored me for a year when I first joined the business school. Amy read my 'super shitty' first book plan, and provided heaps of valuable and honest feedback that made this book possible. Amy also sets a great example as a thought leader, and I often heard myself asking, 'What would Amy do in this situation?' Thank you, Amy, for trusting me and guiding me through my personal upgrade.

Writing a book about upgrading inner operating systems, including mine, was a surreal process. I'm forever indebted to my clients who agreed to share their stories. Thank you for being the inspiration and the foundation for this book.

Turning an idea into a book is much harder than it sounds; the process is both challenging and rewarding. I want to thank the people involved in the process who helped make this happen.

Thank you to my book coach, Kelly Irving. I cannot find the right words to describe Kelly's immense expertise and her keen insights, which shaped the structure of this book.

A special thank you to Carolyn Jackson for your editorial efforts, ongoing support and encouragement, and for making my messy mind as eloquent as possible on paper. Thank you to all the team at Grammar Factory Publishing, including Ania for coordinating the complex process and Julia for designing the cover – I love how eye-catching it is – and Dania for the beautiful interior design that makes it so easy to read! Thank you Scott MacMillan, the most patient and supportive publishing manager I could ever hope for.

Thank you to Wayne, a super talented independent illustrator, who sketched all the pictures and diagrams in the book. Thank you for being so passionate about your work/hobby. I absolutely love those little robots who obviously experienced the upgrade themselves.

Finally, major thanks to all the people who played a role in my journey to get here!

Thanks to my friends, Grace and Sophia, for being the people I could turn to during my dark and desperate years and who supported me in waking up spiritually in Bahai Faith. Thanks to Glenn and Clair for opening my mind to spirituality, leadership and management! Appreciations also go to Helen and Paul for pointing me to organisational learning and development when I struggled to find a career path that combines my innate talent, passion and calling.

Thank you, Nawa and Ju, for trusting me wholeheartedly and believing in me more than I did myself. I am thankful to have you in my life.

To my families – my parents and sister – thank you for allowing me the space to be different, and thank you for putting up with me when I was weird and rebellious! Thank you to my goddaughter Chloe for teaching me valuable life lessons of being open to challenges and leading a life full of joy, and thank you for being such a great inspiration in my life. Thank you Sally and Gordon for keeping me grounded and connected all the time.

Huge thanks to my friends, mentors and beta readers: Alex, Glenn, John, Col, Paul, Delia, Richard, Emily, Karen and Afsaneh. Thank you for your moral support and endless deep conversations that opened my mind and shifted my perspectives. Thank you for crossing paths with me and making my journey of self-discovery and growth full of meaningful moments.

Introduction

....

Your inner strength is your outer foundation.

— ALLAN RUFUS

....

Before I started to write this book, the news came that one of my most admired entrepreneurs, Tony Hsieh, the founder of Zappos and the author of *Delivering Happiness: A Path to Profits, Passion, and Purpose*, had passed away at the age of forty-six due to 'excessive drug use'.

For those who are not familiar with him, here is a snapshot of Tony:

Tony Hsieh was the son of Taiwanese immigrants and born in Urbana, Illinois. He graduated from Harvard at the age of twenty-two and founded his first online business, networking site LinkExchange, at twenty-three. Within three years he had sold it to Microsoft for $265 million. Tony joined Zappos as CEO in 1999, when he was twenty-six, and grew the company's sales from $1.6 million in 2000 to $1 billion by 2009. Later, he sold Zappos to Amazon for $1.2 billion, but remained as CEO until 2021, a few months before his death.

Looking in from the outside, the story of Hsieh's career paints an image of a man whose mission in life was to create happiness. He was driven by his fervour for purpose and passion in life. He was not just a successful innovator, but someone who wanted to improve the human condition. He made 'employees' happiness' Zappos's top priority, he provided financial support to his employees to enable them to actualise their dreams and potential outside the business, and he inspired many leaders globally to shift their views on happiness and profit. Personally, however, he was struggling.

Leading a purposeful, visionary and inspiring life often comes with a package full of stress, frustration, anxiety and loneliness... If you want to be the first person to stand out from the crowd and lead, you also have to have the ability to handle all those strong emotions and difficult situations. You need to pay special attention to your mental health and your inner world. I believe Tony Hsieh failed to do this.

Unfortunately, Tony's personal struggles took a dramatic turn south over the final year of his life, especially as the COVID-19 pandemic curtailed the non-stop action that he seemingly craved. Living a highly demanding and stressful life, Tony developed inappropriate coping strategies. He became a heavy drinker and veered into frequent drug use, inhaling nitrous oxide cartridges to help his struggles with sleep and feelings of loneliness. He distanced himself from friends who tried to put interventions in place to get him sober. Instead, he retreated to Park City, where he surrounded himself with 'yes' men, paying them double to 'be happy' with him, which meant encouraging his drug use, either tacitly or actively. Tony died in a house fire in Connecticut, and while speculation surrounds the exact cause of the fire, there is evidence to suggest that his use of nitrous oxide was involved.

Tony Hsieh inspired millions with his zest for life, and people fell in love with his humanity. But in the end, what used to be his strength became his weakness.

We all want to feel successful in our personal and professional lives. It feels good to be successful – whether that's increasing the profits of the company we work for, being promoted to the top of the corporate ladder, or having our family and friends tell us how loved and valued we make them feel.

Tony Hsieh was an inspiring business leader. You might think that his stratospheric career trajectory was the very definition of success. So why did he get involved in drugs and surround himself with 'yes' people? Why couldn't he sleep? Why was he lonely? Surely his success must have given him deep, personal contentment? His life might have looked aspirational from the outside, but it's what was inside that really mattered. Tony's success was external – if he had been deeply fulfilled on a personal level, he wouldn't have sought comfort in drugs and the company of 'yes' men.

What about you? What is your definition of success? Is your business going the way you want it to? Or do you recognise yourself in some of the following scenarios?

The more you do, the more anxious you get
Are you more of a 'human doing' than a 'human being'? Do you wake up with a long list of tasks to do, and is your self-esteem challenged if there's a blank day on your calendar? Do you refuse

to stop until you have literally used your last bit of energy to complete your to-do list?

More importantly, does completing the list make you feel fulfilled? We may feel satisfied that we did what we set out to do, but fulfilment is a totally different thing. It doesn't come from **what** we do, it comes from **why** we do what we do. And why we do what we do comes from inside us – from **who** we truly are, not the person that others perceive us to be.

The more you achieve, the emptier you feel

Tony Hsieh was surely not the only leader who fought battles between outer achievement and inner emptiness. In the business world, there are plenty of executives who appear to be successful on the surface – who have degrees from prestigious universities, who hold positions with huge responsibilities and big, fat pay cheques, who win awards and titles – but who are deeply unhappy inside. It's as if the more successful they become externally, the more unhappy they feel internally. They feel empty. Perhaps you do, too.

So, what do we do when we feel empty? Many of us try to fill the emptiness with drugs, alcohol or luxury items and more bright, shining titles and rewards. But none of these things will fill the empty hole, because they all come from outside. You must fill this hole from the inside.

The more successful you become, the more your ego takes over

Bill Walsh once brilliantly said, 'Ego is when self-confidence becomes arrogance.' Unlike confidence, the ego operates out of perceived self-interest. The main job ego does is to protect us, to make us feel good and look good, and it does so by seeking approval and validation at all costs. What matters to ego is that we must be seen as 'right', and we must be better than others. All of this is external – about how you appear to others – because the ego can only be satisfied from the outside in.

Ego is the primary reason leaders fail. It is the reason Tony Hsieh failed; he surrounded himself with 'yes' men to keep his ego happy, and when ego gets in the way, brilliant leaders forget that they are there to serve others.

The more driven you are, the more you lose yourself

As Peter Drucker said, 'No measurement, no improvement.' This is true both in business and in life. When meeting business leaders, I always ask: 'What does success mean to you? How do you measure it?' I always get the same answers: 'The projects I did ... the money I made ... the number of people who reported to me ... the market share ... the number of connections we made ... ' to name just a few. But these are all external measures.

When we only measure success by external factors, we copy and use others' standards and miss the opportunity to celebrate **WHY** we do **WHAT** we do **HOW** we do it. This is how we join the rat race and lose our unique identities. When we ONLY set our eyes on external milestones, we forget to lead self, and this is a key reason why driven leaders fail.

The higher you climb, the further you fall

Have you noticed that success tends to be inconsistent and often fleeting? That it comes to you momentarily, and then reality throws you a curve ball and brings you down again? So many of us are trapped in this cycle of reaching a peak only to drop to the bottom, then climb up again, and then drop down again... You find yourself asking why circumstances keep getting in the way of sustained, long-lasting success.

But circumstances don't just happen. Quite often, we create them from within – they are the result of the thoughts we have about ourselves. Our thoughts have much more influence on our success than we are aware of. They drive the emotions and actions that produce the results!

SUCCESS COMES FROM WITHIN

If you want to change your reality, you need to start from the inside out. Working on your internal operating systems will help you avoid all the traps described earlier, and put you on a steady, consistent path towards meaningful success.

To understand how all this works, let's consider how a human being resembles an iceberg, which explains, in a simple way, why people do what they do the way they do it.

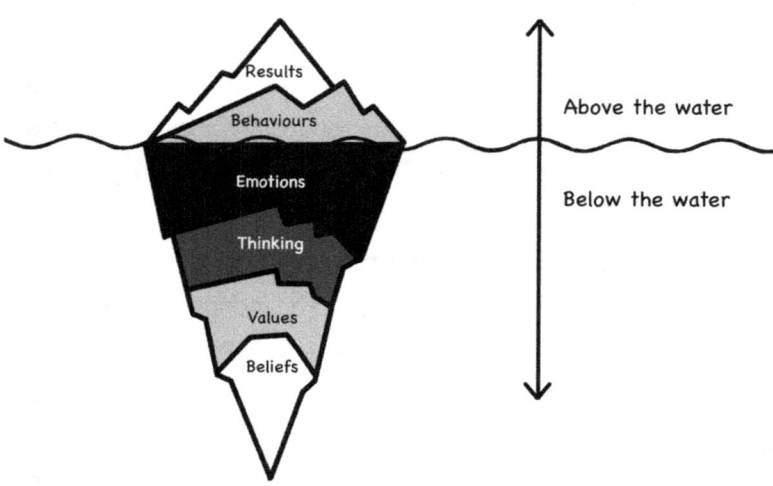

Figure 1: Iceberg of human

6

As you can see from this figure, there are parts of us that can be seen by others, and parts of us that are hidden from others. Those parts that are hidden from others are, most of the time, also hidden from ourselves.

The parts of us that can be observed by others are our behaviours – what we do or did. They can be one-off things, such as losing our temper in a meeting with colleagues, or habitual things we do all the time, such as driving to the office the same way every day. This part of us is represented by the part of the iceberg that is above the waterline.

All our behaviours produce results, some of which might be what we want, and some of which might not be. For example, losing our temper in a meeting with colleagues might produce an undesirable result – that of being perceived as a dictator. But driving to the office the same way every day would surely produce the desired result of arriving at work.

Basically, whatever we do, consciously or unconsciously, planned or unplanned, occasionally or consistently, as long we do it, it will produce results. The trick is to make sure those results are the ones we want. If we deliberately choose and design our behaviours, the results they produce will be the ones we want. These are what we call achievements.

But often we behave in ways that are not in alignment with the results we desire, and this is when we sabotage ourselves! For example, you might want to be perceived as an inspiring leader, but you won't achieve this if you keep losing your temper in meetings.

So, what drives us to choose behaviours that produce undesirable results? To understand that, we must look below the waterline.

The first two layers underneath the waterline are the drivers of our behaviours – emotions and thoughts. That is, what we feel and what we think. By looking at the diagram, you can see that actions – including behaviours that do not serve us – are triggered by our emotions.

Which begs the question: What triggers emotions? The answer? Thoughts!

And what triggers thoughts? Values and beliefs.

It is these parts of yourself that are hidden from others – and sometimes yourself – that are the keys to your external success. I call this underwater operation your 'inner operating system' (IOS). It is these below-the-waterline aspects of yourself that automatically and unconsciously produce the results that you have to live with. If you want to be successful, you need to work on yourself from the inside out, which means working on your inner operating system (IOS).

Unless you consciously review and upgrade your inner operating systems, you may not be able to gain the results you desire sustainably – you may find that any success is short-lived. This book is about understanding and upgrading your inner operating systems, your 'below the waterline' operation, so that your 'above the waterline' deliveries – your external behaviours and actions – can produce the results you desire – in the short term as well as the long term.

Let me introduce you to your **IOS** – your inner operating system.

MEET YOUR IOS

Your IOS is essentially the below-the-waterline part of yourself. In a sense, your underwater operation is your BEING, and the above-the-water operation is your DOING. Now let's dive a bit deeper...

Your IOS is made up of four systems, which are interconnected. Each system supports, influences and affects the other three. Those four systems, and their 'jurisdictions', are:

- Mental Operating System (MOS): Your MOS is in charge of your thoughts, beliefs and worldview.
- Spiritual Operating System (SOS): Your SOS is in charge of your values, character, purpose and meaning.
- Emotional Operating System (EOS): Your EOS is in charge of your feelings, attitudes and actions.
- Physical Operating System (POS): Your POS is in charge of your energy, strength and stamina.

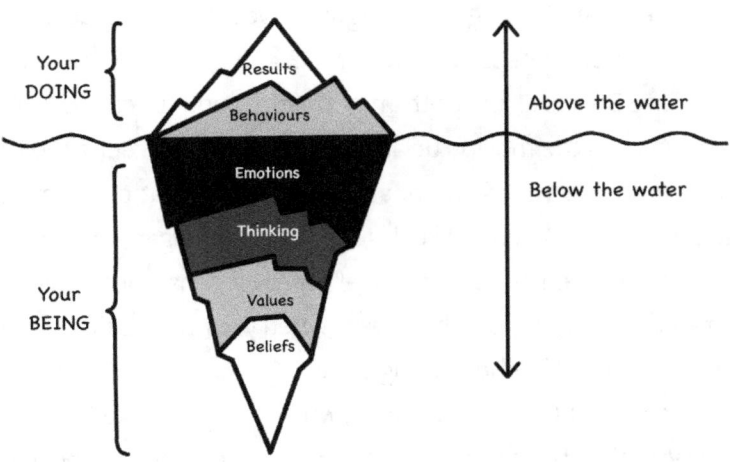

Figure 2: Iceberg

To illustrate how this IOS works, it's helpful to think of a sailing boat. Each of us is like a sailing boat, navigating the seas of life, and for a safe and smooth journey we need all four systems up and running at their best.

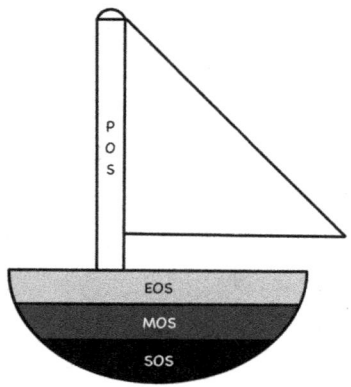

Figure 3: Sailing boat

Looking at the diagram in Figure 3, you can see that the hull of the boat comprises your SOS, MOS and EOS.

Your SOS sits at the bottom of the boat and functions like the keel, which is the most crucial part of the boat. It keeps the boat straight and serves as the boat's 'spinal cord' that connects the parts together. When the keel is broken or damaged, the boat will capsize. A broken or damaged keel usually means a dead ship. The same concept applies to humans – when your SOS is not running properly, we're like the walking dead.

Above the SOS sits your MOS, which functions like the navigation system of the boat. We use it to find direction and be aware of other boats around us, the surroundings. It helps us to assess circumstances and to make decisions and choices. We rely on our MOS to collect the right data to make informed decisions.

Above the MOS sits your EOS, which functions like the rudder of your boat. It steers the boat and is sensitive to misalignment and water pressure. While sailing, the rudder is sometimes visible and sometimes invisible. A fast, smoothly sailing boat depends on how well the captain can control the rudder – it's either lifted up and steering the boat, or creating more resistance in the water to slow down the boat. Just like in humans, our emotions either lift us up or crush us down.

Finally, we have the mast of the boat, which is the big pole that stands on the deck and connects the sail to the boat. The stronger the mast is, the better it can hold the sail and harness the wind. The mast represents your POS, and just like the mast of a boat, if you keep your physical body clean, solid and strong, it will give you the best chance to survive and thrive.

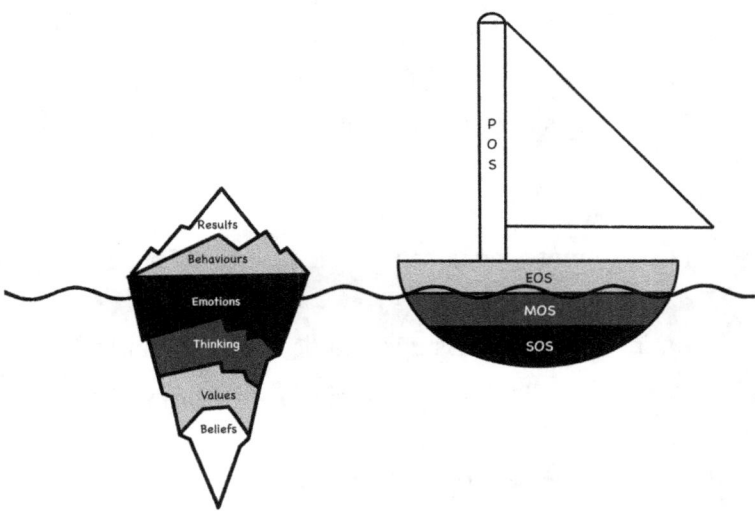

Figure 4: Iceberg and boat

Together, the four individual systems that make up your IOS have an impact on your overall performance, and each has an influence on the others. But they don't just automatically perform at their optimal level all the time without any attention from you. Just like a sailing boat on a long voyage, each part of the system needs to be checked and upgraded regularly to ensure you can go the distance. Running a business is a long voyage.

Like any system, an older and outdated IOS creates poor performance. Vital data are missing, more mistakes are made, and more time and energy are spent on fixing problems instead of doing what is necessary to move forward. Even if just one operating system is outdated, it not only impairs its own performance but also undermines the performance of the other systems and, therefore, your overall performance.

The symptoms you may experience when these operating systems are not upgraded and up to date include:

- Finding it challenging to influence others, even though you have achieved a lot financially.
- Feeling constantly burned out, or experiencing significantly impaired health that prevents you from doing what you want to do.
- Feeling empty and unhappy inside, despite having achieved a lot.
- Running into endless ups and downs, constantly fighting for survival ... and experiencing endless emotional turmoils.

However, if you take time to review and upgrade these inner operating systems, chances are that growth and sustained success will come your way. You will be able to achieve more – and more easily. You will not only be able to make a profit, but also make a difference. Most importantly, you will be able to stay true to who you are when you become successful. Unlike Tony Hsieh, your success will come from inside, from your being, not just from what you gained externally.

So, how do we upgrade these inner operating systems? That's what this book is about. It will take you through each of your four inner operating systems and explain what they are in charge of and how they work and, most importantly, how to upgrade them.

UPGRADING YOUR IOS

Unlike upgrading an operating system on your smartphone or computer, which only requires you to press the 'update' button, upgrading your inner operating system requires three steps:

Step 1: Understand your default settings

Each of your inner operating systems has default settings – your habitual ways of thinking, feeling and doing. It feels comfortable and effortless to conduct ourselves on our default settings. But while operating on default settings, we are simply repeating what we have done in the past. And if we keep doing what we have always done, it is guaranteed that we will only get the results we've always got.

A truly successful person is the one who constantly and regularly upgrades their default settings manually and uses their operating systems to their full potential. Someone who takes the easy way out and keeps bumbling along on their default settings will find themselves complaining that life is hard and unfair.

The most critical moment of your life is when you realise that examining and adjusting your default settings is the only path to growth. Awareness of your default settings, your ability to evaluate them, and your willingness to upgrade them are the key components of growing into your life fully! Upgrading your inner operating system is not a job that everyone does automatically. It requires courage and discipline to shift yourself out of your default settings.

Step 2: Plug in new beliefs

Beliefs are the things that are not necessarily true, but that we hold to be true. They are subjective. They represent an acceptance that someone or something – an idea or a concept – exists or is right, even without proof.

For instance, if you grew up with parents who didn't show emotions such as affection or appreciation, you may have developed the belief that expressing emotions such as gratitude or appreciation is unnecessary. You may feel uncomfortable praising others or giving public recognition to your team.

The problem is that many of our beliefs are not conscious – that's right, we are not even aware of them. We are not aware of what they are, or whether they are useful for us or are limiting us. In the second step of upgrading your IOS, you will discard limiting beliefs and replace them with new beliefs that will expand your vision, enable you to perceive situations differently, and empower you to grow.

Step 3: Embody new practices

Success is not about what we do occasionally; it's about what we do consistently. The third step in upgrading your IOS is to take up new practices and do that consistently. To enable consistency, we use repetition.

If we repeat often and consistently enough, we achieve or even overshoot our goals. When you are in the process of upgrading your inner operating systems, embodied practices play a vital role to help systems running on upgraded software function smoothly and without extra effort.

In the chapters that follow, you will find practices that are designed to ensure that you can intentionally influence your brain and behaviour in a positive way. Through such practices, the self-upgrading eventually becomes automatic.

WHAT DO I KNOW?

You may be wondering how I know all this. The answer is that I learnt these lessons the hard way. My mid-life crisis started when I was twenty-two. That year, I graduated from university, passed the bar examination, and started to work in a government agency as a junior legal officer.

Working in the legal industry had been my dream since high school. I should have been happy as that dream finally came true. But I was not. I was miserable and depressed as my beliefs system collapsed in just six months. It was like everything I learnt while growing up had flipped upside down. Many things I held true were crushed by reality. Suddenly, honesty was not considered a virtue. On the contrary, being truthful was considered naive and immature. Speaking up for people who are not able to speak for themselves was thought to be stupid and was discouraged. At the age of twenty-two, I felt like I'd been living a lie for my whole life, and I was stuck in this giant machine that was creating and covering up more lies. I felt like I needed to cut off half of myself to fit into the system and gain worldly approval. But did I want to? NO! I didn't want to. But I couldn't articulate why I didn't want to; I only knew something inside of me needed to break out, and I didn't know what it was.

So I started a journey to get to know myself. It was a process that involved changing jobs, changing countries, and even changing my circle of friends. But the more I began to focus on looking inside to see what was going on, the more clarity I got.

I discovered that the way I was thinking was deeply flawed. I jumped to conclusions, I made biased judgements, and I criticised myself to the point that I firmly believed I was not capable of doing anything my heart desired.

I discovered that I hated my emotions. As an empathetic and sensitive person, my everyday life was like an emotional roller coaster, and that exhausted me. Growing up in a family that only felt comfortable expressing anger and sorrow, I felt awkward when meeting my other emotions.

I also discovered that the busier I made myself and the more goals I actualised, the emptier and more hollow I felt. By pushing myself hard, all the energy in me was sucked away … I was occupied, but was I fulfilled?

After these discoveries, I embarked on a decade of 'fixing' myself. The word 'fixing' might sound unkind, but there were moments when I felt like I was using a tiny screwdriver and adjusting myself bit by bit until I could once again operate at full capacity and, more importantly, do so without burning myself out or limiting myself.

I worked for decades in corporate as a learning and development executive, and I specialised in providing solutions to develop and grow people's capabilities. I witnessed the struggles and challenges faced by employees and leaders at all levels. And I learnt that how far a person can go and how well they can uplift their capabilities to do their job all comes down to one thing: are they capable of upgrading their inner operating systems?

So, my friend, if you have been busy chasing goals and achieving milestones, and if, from time to time, you have that feeling that all those worldly achievements are losing their power to make you excited, then take this book as my gift to you. It will help you to find yourself and upgrade yourself. That's right, you don't need to 'fix' yourself; instead, learn from my experience how to automatically upgrade yourself and tap into your superpowers – superpowers that will help you to lead a meaningful and successful life from the inside out!

IS THIS BOOK FOR YOU?

When running your business, do you do it as a job, a career or a calling?

- When it's a **job**, you exchange your time for the pay, and the business is mainly a source of income that pays for your life outside the business.
- When it is a **career**, you don't settle for the income it brings, but you seek out opportunities to expand yourself and advance the business. You have a long-term vision for your business, and set up goals and work on actualising them.
- When running a business is a **calling** for you, you feel much deeper alignment between the business and who you are as a person. You are passionate about what you are doing, you have a strong sense of purpose, and you are mission oriented. You are willing to work hard to grow and contribute, and in turn you experience the highest level of satisfaction and fulfilment from running your business.

Which one applies to you?

This is a book written to support business leaders who want **MORE!**

One of the fundamental beliefs that I hold close to my heart when offering my services to the world is that we are everything, and everything and everyone are interconnected. What we think, feel and do always has consequences, which may impact ourselves, the people around us, and people we don't know or cannot reach in our lifetime.

Unfortunately, too often, this is overlooked.

This is a book written for people who want to intervene in this chain of events and take back control of the impact they make. It supports leaders and organisations to upgrade their inner operating systems so that they can navigate complexities and uncertainties with more ease, leverage the power of the unknown and uncertain to unfold and create, and seek within to utilise all their resources to optimise outcomes.

Leaders and organisations who are inspired to bring clarity, focus and creativity into their daily practices can optimise their performance by upgrading their inner operating systems, and maximise their positive impact with ease.

WHAT TO EXPECT

The path to achieve outwardly starts from the journey to upgrade the inner self.

When you start a business, you have a vision as to what that business can bring to your life. You desire success in business so that you can enjoy a fulfilling and abundant life. These two things go hand in hand.

When you are worried that everything might go wrong in your business, and that worry becomes your focus, your business will suffer right along with you. But if you go to work every day knowing that business is a series of circumstances and situations that can all be handled, and with the attitude that there is always a way to solve the problems, your business will be a reflection of that mindset too.

Changing yourself as a business leader depends on your ability to examine yourself, to notice your thinking-feeling-doing patterns and, most importantly, to review and fine-tune your inner operating systems. Helping you to do that are what the following pages are all about.

Regardless of the business you are in, you are your first product, and you will always be that first product. That first product produces future products – your business and your services. You may learn the best strategy in the market, but how you apply those strategies is your personal touch, which comes from who you are. You are the very first product you developed, and it is your choice whether this product will continue to evolve or stay stuck in its first iteration.

Your business success depends on your ability to upgrade yourself. When you own the business, everything is your responsibility.

You have the power and authority to solve any problem that comes to your door. When your business has a problem, be bold enough to accept it's your responsibility and that you can change it.

Change is a must for business.

But, before changing your marketing strategy, before hiring

new people, before developing a new product, before signing up new alliances ... reserve time and energy to change yourself. This is a MUST, because YOU attract the problems your business encounters. Your external world only mirrors your internal world.

Are you ready?

Let's go!

Chapter 1
Mental Operating System

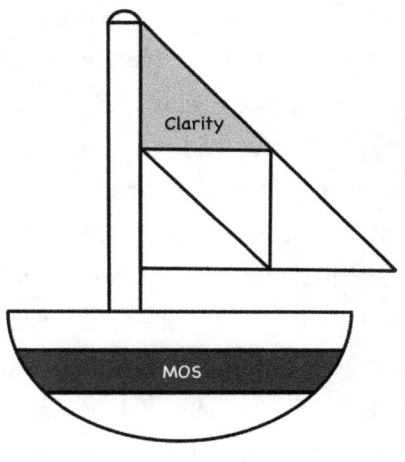

Bella is a smart, brave and hard-working business owner. She started her business right out of school, in an industry that is labour intensive and where success is mainly measured by material gains.

In the early days of her business, Bella quickly learnt how to survive in the industry. But while hard work is all very well, she barely had any personal time and the only 'ME' time she could afford was going on a shopping spree after completing a big project. She also found herself playing in the grey areas … she developed 'beneficial relationships' with 'influential people' by giving them what they needed. Sometimes they needed something but would prefer that no one ever knew about it. Bella's ability to fulfil these 'needs' brought her opportunities to expand her business.

Bella is action oriented and has always been proud of herself for making quick decisions to solve problems. She doesn't mind getting involved in the practical side of the business and rolling up her sleeves to help get the job done. She's proud that monitoring all the work done by her people has ensured the quality of their projects. She's also proud that she single-handedly created a multi-million dollar business and is surrounded by people who worship her.

But lately, Bella has hit several walls – all without warning. Some investors walked away. Some employees walked away and joined her competitors … and she went back to working long hours and eating and sleeping in the office, just like she did when she started the business.

When she came to me, Bella couldn't stop talking or complaining about how unfair the world was. She gave herself 100 per cent to the business, she put her heart and soul into making it profitable for everyone, she treated her employees and investors generously, but in the end she was betrayed. She couldn't think straight, couldn't figure out what had gone wrong, and wondered whether this was the normal path of being a successful business owner.

Meet your mind

In this chapter, we will focus on the mental operating system (**MOS**) that runs our internal world, and which is in charge of our thoughts, beliefs and world view, and has an impact on our emotions. I want to start with the mind because all the knowledge workers I've worked with consider the mind to be a person's greatest asset.

What we call the 'mind' comprises patterns of thoughts and feelings that are repeated throughout our lives. These patterns are largely unconscious and operate automatically. A poorly operating MOS can really paralyse your willpower and your desire to do things. Only strategic and constant work will improve your thoughts. Better thoughts will bring more positive actions, and more positive actions will bring more positive outcomes. It's that simple. Your way of thinking defines your way of doing things and interacting with the world.

The hardware that your MOS runs on is your brain. The major job your brain does is to keep you alive – to make sure you can survive. All the complicated functionalities run by the brain are there to ensure we are safe. Regardless of the situation, the brain will use its knowledge, experiences and preferences to select the action for us to take that is most likely to keep us safe, physically and psychologically. If there's a cliff in front of us, our brain stops us from moving forward. It also stops us from making a fool of ourselves by telling us that what we are attempting to do is wrong ... so we stay where we are, because it is safe.

The fact that our brains keep us safe is good news, but the downside is that its need to keep us safe by all means can limit us in certain ways. The brain wants us to feel comfortable, and comfort comes from familiarity. As long as we repeat ourselves, the brain is happy. But repeating ourselves comfortably can sabotage our ability to grow and progress.

It's helpful to understand the role of beliefs here. We can think of beliefs as the software that our brain runs. We observe, assess and interpret the world and ourselves through the filters of our beliefs. This is a process that happens 24/7, and we don't have much conscious control over it. Most of the time, we don't even notice its existence.

One of the most popular and important quotes in history, attributed to Mahatma Gandhi, goes like this:

....

Your beliefs become your thoughts, your thoughts become your words, your words become your actions, your actions become your habits, your habits become your values and your values become your destiny.

....

It's a causal analysis that shows very well how your thoughts shape your destiny. The problem in this causality or, to be more exact, between your thoughts and your destiny, is the untamed human mind. Your beliefs affect your thoughts, and your unchecked thought patterns reinforce your beliefs.

Our MOS determines how we feel about the outside world, not the other way around. So rather than trying to improve our lives and create happiness by controlling the outside world, we need to work on our MOS.

But most of us are not educated on how to monitor, regulate or upgrade our MOS. We don't know how to observe the operation of the MOS so that we can make changes that drive the behaviour that helps us achieve what we desire. We don't know how to upgrade our thinking-feeling-behaving patterns.

HOW THE MOS WORKS

It helps to understand the operational process of our MOS. On one level, the MOS works when neurons work. The neuron is the smallest cell in the brain, and works by releasing brain chemicals, known as neurotransmitters, that generate electrical signals in neighbouring neurons. This is how thoughts and actions are generated.

The lives we have, our daily routines, the situations we encounter at home, at work and in relationships all trigger patterns of neuronal firing, which results in a thought process. When neurons fire in the same way over and over again, it reinforces the circuitry. Patterns are formed, shortcuts created, habits shaped.

Now let's take our understanding deeper by introducing a key model: the Ladder of Inference. This model was created by Chris Argyris in 1970, and describes the stages of the thinking process we go through to make decisions and choose actions based on the facts we observe.

The ladder has seven rungs, and works from the bottom up:

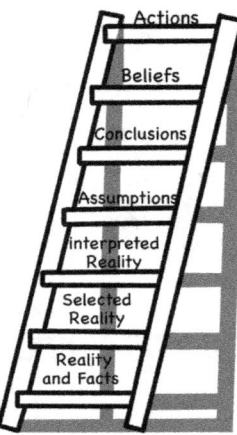

Figure 5: Ladder of Inference

1. The first rung is **reality and facts** – what's in the environment outside of us.
2. The second rung is **selected reality**, or how we experience the reality and pay attention to certain facts over others based on our beliefs and previous experiences.
3. The third rung is **interpreted reality**. Here, we interpret what the facts of a situation mean according to our beliefs and preferences.
4. The fourth rung is about **assumptions**. This is where we form assumptions, often without thinking.
5. On the fifth rung, we draw **conclusions** according to the interpreted facts and assumptions.
6. The sixth rung is where we either form or reinforce the **beliefs** based on the conclusions and assumptions.

7. The seventh rung represents the 'right' and 'appropriate' **action** we take based on the beliefs we have formed.

In reality, you might think your mind doesn't work this way at all – you don't have to go through five steps to draw a conclusion. Most of the time, our conclusions or understanding of a situation seem obvious to us and we tend to skip the rungs to make the 'best' choice of actions.

On the one hand, skipping steps is essential for survival and thriving. It saves us a tremendous amount of time and energy in making decisions. On the other hand, it is flawed and may create a vicious loop that traps us. Because the beliefs we hold directly affect the reality we perceive, we tend to select the facts relevant to our beliefs and leave the rest out when making decisions. Very soon, we start jumping to conclusions based on assumptions.

In Bella's case, she believed that people who slept in the office worked diligently and gave their all to the business, so she encouraged that behaviour. She also believed that people who liked to socialise with her, made her the centre of the attention and did what they were told were the most loyal employees and should be rewarded. So some employees made it the priority to come to her weekly get-together to have free meals and fun with the boss after work or on weekends. But employees who have a family and life outside work, who didn't have time to come to the get-togethers, felt left out. They'd find that they didn't always understand the jokes the others talked about, and eventually felt excluded from Bella's inner circle, which led them to leave the business eventually as they didn't feel this is the place they belong to. So, you can see here how Bella's beliefs influenced her actions and ultimately the fate of her business.

When filtering information from the outside world, we tend to omit, distort and generalise. We pay selective attention and notice some of the data, but we overlook or omit others; we then interpret the data according to our experiences and add layers of misrepresentations of reality. Have you ever been scared by a 'snake', then discovered it was just a piece of rope? We tend to generalise and draw global conclusions based on the limited experiences we have had.

DEFAULT SETTINGS OF THE MOS

If you're struggling in business, it's probably not due to a lack of effort. A great number of business leaders put blood, sweat and tears into their work, but still end up wondering where things went wrong. After being in business for ten years, Bella had had her peak moments and bought several properties, but had to sell out to save the business – twice.

Many leaders have the best intentions and put in their best effort to make their dreams come true, but the default settings of their MOS repeatedly pull them down to the ground.

Let's look at some of the common default settings I have observed in business leaders.

Fixed mindset

Our mindset is a habitual way of thinking that influences what we do and what we experience.

Carol Dweck, a researcher at Stanford University, is well known for her work on the 'fixed' and 'growth' mindset. In her bestseller book, *Mindset*, she describes the difference between these two mindsets and how they impact our performance:

> 'In a fixed mindset students believe their basic abilities, their intelligence, their talents, are just fixed traits. They have a certain amount and that's that, and then their goal becomes to look smart all the time and never look dumb. In a growth mindset students understand that their talents and abilities can be developed through effort, good teaching and persistence. They don't necessarily think everyone's the same or anyone can be Einstein, but they believe everyone can get smarter if they work at it.'[1]

Many of us have a fixed mindset in certain situations. This may prevent important skill development and growth, which in turn can sabotage our performance.

Let's return to Bella's story to see how a fixed mindset may have contributed to the problems in her business.

> In conversations with Bella, she repeatedly said, 'I gave them so much money, and they still betrayed me!'
>
> 'Do you know what truly motivated them?' I asked.
>
> 'Money, of course! Who doesn't like money?'
>
> 'How do you know for sure? Do you know what they care about the most outside of work?'
>
> 'I don't know! I'm not a people person or a conversationalist, and I don't have time to chit chat!'

If you say, 'I'm not a people person,' or 'I'm not good at having conversations,' your fixed mindset is coming out. The reason it is called 'fixed' is that it makes you feel there is nothing you can do about it. The way you think is all set in stone and you cannot change it. A fixed mindset hinders our ability to learn, grow and develop new skills.

On the other hand, someone with a growth mindset wouldn't see their lack of skills as a hurdle. They would practise people skills and take actions that led to authentic bonding via meaningful conversations. They would create opportunities to communicate and connect with people, even if they feel awkward at first. In fact, they would see awkwardness, through practise, as the path to ease.

If you are a business owner, it's very likely that you have an undiscovered fixed mindset in certain aspects of your work that makes you feel stuck, or even self-sabotaged as Bella did. Are you aware of yours?

Scarcity mindset

A scarcity mindset is the state or feeling of not having enough of something, of believing that we need something more to have a happy and fulfilled life.

A lot of people run their business with a scarcity mindset. They believe that there is only a limited quantity of resources, money and opportunities available in the universe. Therefore, they believe that they have to compete, by all means possible, for customers, business opportunities, market attention, fame and status.

When we're running our business with a scarcity mindset, hard work isn't enough to succeed because we are pouring all our effort into doing the wrong things instead of seizing the opportunities that really matter that will grow our business. We get muddled in details and minutiae.

In the conversations I had with Bella, I discovered that she had a scarcity mindset. Given how competitive her industry is, she constantly feared that her bright, hard-to-find talents would leave her for her competitors. So, she closely monitored their work and watched every single move they made. Her staff were required to manually record their work activity every fifteen minutes – not for billing purposes, but so that she could review what they were doing. Bella was also the only one who had the authority to approve expenses in the business, so any invoice over $150 had to get her signature.

Most of the time, a scarcity mindset is driven by fear and anxiety, which blocks your creativity and either makes you chase easy wins or leads you to avoid challenges and difficulties. This doesn't just keep you small and 'safe', but also obscures positive thinking and personal expansion. When it comes to running a business in competitive markets, we can easily worry about where the next client will be coming from or become anxious about a lack of funds to pay bills and salaries. When we are caught up by these limiting beliefs, it's not surprising that we can start to behave in the following ways:

- Refuse to pay employees fairly or generously, and hold all the money in hand.
- Refuse to praise or appreciate others.
- Refuse to delegate and empower employees, and instead dictate and micromanage.
- Refuse to invest in training and developing self and others, but believe you know it all and that your way is the only way.
- Refuse to share your thoughts and resources, and refuse to support and collaborate with others if you cannot be the winner, as if you can only win when others lose, but then resent others' success.

The most successful business leaders function with an abundance mindset.

Abundance is the state or feeling of plentifulness. Business leaders with an abundance mindset believe that there are unlimited resources, opportunities, money, relationships and success available in the universe, and that there are enough of these for everyone.

So, instead of focusing on competition, leaders who are driven by an abundance mindset focus more on seeking opportunities. They invest in themselves and their people; they see the value in personal and professional development; they prioritise resources to provide growth opportunities as much as possible; they see difficulties and obstacles as opportunities for learning and growth; and they share, they like to contribute, and they enable others to be more successful! They come with an attitude of gratitude, they appreciate others honestly and generously, they are open-minded, and they inspire kind contributions.

Which is your default setting?

Short-termism

Many small businesses exhibit short-termism – the tendency to focus on the short term and ignore (or largely overlook) the long term. When I asked Bella: 'Do your people have a shared vision of the business?' she replied, 'We are busy with the many projects we have in hand, so our vision is to finish those projects within the timeframe promised.' Which is not wrong, but it is not right either.

When your business is small, you also tend to think small. For example, you tend to always pick the cheapest solution instead of the best. You might hire the cheapest talent instead of the most suitable to save operational costs, and then not spend a single cent on employee capability development. This can lead to spending more time and energy on correcting mistakes, which will hurt the business in the long run.

It is true that we need to consider short-term effectiveness, and short-term measures are effective at getting employees focused on specific targets. It is also true, however, that if you have a vision about the contribution your business can make to society during, and even after, your time here, you will attract different people to work with you, and money won't be the one and only tool to motivate them.

Unfortunately, way too many smart and diligent business leaders spend all their time and energy focusing on the now, with little or no regard for the future, and make decisions and take actions to fulfil immediate needs only.

For example, instead of outsourcing services, they do everything themselves regardless of whether it's their forte: marketing, sales, graphic designing, even data entry ... all to save on operational costs. But when they bury themselves in this detailed work, they have no mental space or energy to think about overall business vision and strategies, not to mention the execution of those strategies.

In Stephen Covey's book *The 7 Habits of Highly Effective People*, habit number two is 'Begin with the end in mind'. This addresses the need to develop an 'outcome-oriented mindset'. What do you want to achieve at the end? Without that in mind, the more effort you make now, the more barriers and hurdles you will create for yourself.

So, what has been your default focus?

Reactive problem solving

Our brain craves patterns, as explained before. It consumes tremendous energy to think and create new ways of doing, so the brain would rather follow the path well travelled. That is, the pattern of thinking that we have developed over time and feels simple, easy, familiar and comfortable.

However, what used to give us the results we wanted also has the potential to harm us when applied in the wrong situation. For example, being decisive and fixing a problem quickly is a skill a business leader must have. But while this has its benefits, it also has its limits.

When you're busy and have many demands on you, but your time is limited, you tend to make fast decisions and act quickly. This is not altogether a bad thing, but this habit can blind us to a thorough view of a situation and prevent us from discovering the root cause of an issue. We are in danger of approaching a situation in a particular way because it looks similar to past problems, but in fact it could be slightly different. This habit can blind us to the patterns we are operating with.

An example is the time that Bella fired her project manager on the spot. The story goes like this:

> When Bella walked in the office at 8 a.m. and noticed the project manager wasn't there, she started to get anxious because they were on a tight deadline to deliver the project. She expected to see that everyone in the office, particularly the project manager, was busy doing the work.
>
> When the project manager came in an hour later, she walked up to his desk, reminded him of the tight project schedule, and without giving him the chance to explain fired

him in front of his team members.

Bella later learnt that the PM was late because his car broke down on the way to work. He had called the receptionist, but she was unable to convey the message to Bella immediately. And when the receptionist saw that Bella was furious, she dared not approach her.

If Bella knew what had happened, would she have chosen the same approach? Probably not. Her MOS was driving her to make a quick decision, with or without accurate data to support it. And while she was proud that she had demonstrated her decisiveness as a leader, this behaviour led her people to conclude that she was a dictator.

Bella is not the only business owner or manager who draws conclusions based on assumptions. Most of our default thinking is formed through our early experiences and blended with the influences of those around us. We copy their thinking patterns, we make similar choices, and we either adjust or stick to those mental modes throughout our life – until it doesn't work anymore. Most of the time, the only way we notice that our pattern or the systems we're using don't work is when we encounter a problem.

The bigger the problem we face, the bigger the system upgrade we need.

Unchecked biased thinking

We all have biases, whether we know it or not. Some biases are subtle, while others are more obvious, but all of them can have an impact on our thinking and decision making. Bias, by itself, is neither good nor bad; it is just the shortcut our brain uses to make choices and decisions. However, unchecked biases can affect us and our decision-making processes in several different ways. They can influence the way we see things and how we react to things we see.

The Director of the NeuroLeadership Institute, David Rock, and his team have shown that humans have more than 150 biases! These biases can be grouped into five categories that can negatively affect leadership and business decisions, using the acronym **SEEDS**:

- **Similarity Bias** — This bias operates when we are naturally and unconsciously drawn to people similar to ourselves.

  We tend to like people who are like us and think the same way we do, and dislike people who are not like us or who think differently from us. This can influence who we choose to spend time with and what we choose to watch or read, and affect how we perceive and treat others.

  As business leaders, this bias influences who you hire, who you promote and who you assign to projects. Have you ever felt the urge to hire someone who graduated from the same school you went to, or who spoke your mother tongue, or who climbed the same mountain you conquered?

- **Expedience Bias** — This bias operates when we prefer to act quickly. As business leaders, we tend to rush to judgement about our people without fully considering all the facts. For example, when we review employees we tend to rely solely on one data point or recommendation instead of gathering a wide array of information.

  I've met many business leaders who have this tendency to rely heavily on gut instinct when making important decisions about their employees. For example, if an employee makes a single mistake, you may decide that they are a bad fit for the organisation and let them go without any further investigation. However, if you take time to identify the root cause, you may find that simply letting go of the 'bad performer' is not necessarily the best solution.

- **Experience Bias** — As business leaders, particularly when we have accumulated experience, we tend to consider our perceptions as comprehensive and objective truth, so we close our minds to perspectives and views that are different from ours.

    Let's take a moment to reflect. When you chair a meeting, do you pressure your people to agree with everything you say because of your previous experience, even if they have expertise you don't have? If this is the case, it's time to check your experience bias!

- **Distance Bias** — As humans, we instinctively prioritise that which is nearby, whether in physical space, time or other domains, and disregard important factors that are further away. Simply put, we tend to focus on things that are in front of our eyes.

    If you still follow old-school performance management practices in your business, you probably review your employees' performance once a year and offer a bonus once a year, right? But when distance bias comes into play, you may only remember what happened recently, not over the full twelve months. Rating your people this way rarely motivates them to perform better; it can actually make it more difficult to engage with them.

    Distance bias can cost us big in business! When COVID

started in China, one of the business leaders I spoke to in Sydney casually dismissed the warning: 'It's in China; it has nothing to do with property development here.' Well, the truth was that COVID had a huge impact on the property development industry here, and affected workers, materials, investment and buyers.

- **Safety Bias** — Humans naturally prefer to avoid loss over taking risks for possible gain. As business leaders, this means we are more motivated to protect the status quo and stay in our comfort zone.

  This bias can lead to missed opportunities, delayed innovation and poor decision making because we focus on protecting the status quo and avoiding risks. Even though we know that risk-taking is necessary for innovation and growth, we struggle to take action because we are so afraid of failing.

Whether we are aware of it or not, each and every one of these biases will affect how we perceive a situation, and how we choose solutions to problems.

Distorted thinking

Because of the way our MOS works, we are in constant danger of thinking in a distorted way. Instead of using all the available facts and data to make decisions, we tend to jump to conclusions. Instead of analysing reality, we tend to interpret information based on our past experiences, preferences and beliefs, and do what is convenient and comfortable.

Here are a few examples of 'distorted thinking' that are quite common in the business leaders I encounter.

All-or-nothing thinking

This is when we see things in black and white, not shades of grey.
For example:

- 'If we cannot sign up that client, then my business cannot be trusted with bigger projects.'
- 'My team always messes things up; I cannot let them make any decisions.'
- 'I will never be able to achieve my goals.'

When you express your thinking using absolute terms, such as 'never' or 'ever', your MOS is processing information with an all-or-nothing pattern. This type of faulty thinking shows your inability to see the alternatives in a situation or possible solutions to a problem.

Discounting the positive

This is when you refuse to acknowledge that the positive things that happen are due to the effort you made, and instead insist that it was good luck or coincidence.
For example:

- You successfully negotiated a big deal, but told yourself it was just good luck.
- Your team member made progress, but instead of appreciating what he/she did well, you lecture him/her on what they could have done better.

'Should' statements

This is when you 'should/must/ought' yourself or others on many things, such as saying or thinking, 'I should have done more exercise,'

'You should chase the deal more diligently,' or 'He should have raised that issue earlier...'

Such statements often create fear and doubt in yourself and others. They can make the person feel guilty about what they have or haven't done and create a sense of inadequacy and of not being 'enough'.

Fortune telling

This is when you predict negative outcomes without factual evidence.

For example:

- 'If we send this proposal out, they will reject us for sure.'
- 'If we throw a party, no one will come.'

So, you see, your mind can lead you to think in many ways that hamper your ability to thrive and flourish as a business leader. And this can all happen without you being aware of it. Can you recognise your own thinking in any of the default patterns we have discussed?

BENEFITS OF UPGRADING YOUR MOS

When your MOS remains on its default settings – when it's not upgraded – you'll be trapped in your thinking errors. You'll be solely reliant on other people to spoon-feed knowledge to you and you'll act irrationally. But if your MOS is upgraded properly, then you can quickly learn anything and analyse situations more objectively and accurately.

Let's now look at how an upgraded MOS benefits your business.

Adaptable, creative and flexible leadership

Cognitive flexibility, by definition, means thinking flexibly. In the business world, it contributes to fast learning, creative problem solving, and effective adaptation and response to fast-changing situations.

To survive and thrive in a fast-changing environment, you need the ability to adapt your thinking and behaviours according to the situations and context. You need to hold multiple concepts and perspectives at the same time, and quickly switch your way of perceiving and thinking. This helps you develop new approaches and connections, and know when to shift and change. This ability will make huge differences in your business performance. With an upgraded MOS, you will be able to see multiple perspectives, be more adaptable, and be able to shift your thinking process and find the path to solutions creatively.

COVID was a great test for business leaders' creativity and adaptability. Those who believed they could not adapt to a new business model often failed, while those who refused to be limited thrived because they quickly adapted to the 'new normal'. For example, during the first lockdown in Sydney, within one week, one of my local fine-dining restaurants shifted their business to providing 'half-cooked home meals' at a more affordable price for busy families working and studying at home, in addition to the usual pricey home delivery meals. After the lockdown, this line of business continued to make a profit for the restaurant. I asked the owner, while ordering a meal on the phone, 'What a brilliant idea – how could you shift the business so quickly?' He replied, 'We like to cook for our customers. The format is not important, as long as we can cook for the customers.'

Thinking critically and creatively means that you can learn from others and you can seek feedback and guidance from professionals, but you do not blindly follow 'gurus' and copy and paste their best practices into your business. Instead, you can challenge and adapt best practices into your business and make them work for you.

Clarity in chaos

Running a business can be messy. The business world is full of uncertainties, and the bigger the business, the more complex its problems become. The term VUCA, an acronym for volatility, uncertainty, complexity and ambiguity, has been used to describe both war zones and the business world. In a VUCA environment, it's hard to make the 'best' decisions. When the market changes so fast that no predictions can be made or patterns discerned, it's hard to know how to go forward.

However, an upgraded MOS enables you to step back, broaden your views, collect more data, connect the dots, identify root causes, think outside of the box, and invest in solving the problems that matter.

When your mind is sharp and working at full capacity, you can identify what your actions deliver to you, to your people, and to the society you are in, which can be the financial freedom gained, the skills and competencies developed, and the services we provided that change the world for the better. When you base your decisions on a cool, calm and collected assessment of the situation in hand and the impact in the future, you are able to find clarity in chaos.

HOW TO UPGRADE YOUR MOS

Before we attempt to upgrade your MOS, let's make a few things clear!

- It requires **courage** to admit that our mind has a default setting.
- It requires **an open mind** to recognise that our beliefs are conditioned by our upbringing and environment.
- It requires **personal responsibility** to accept that our thought patterns are our choice, and that we are in complete control of how we think and act.

Upgrading is not easy, but the good news is that the moment we are aware that we have a choice, we will notice that our actions tend to be more conscious and less reactionary.

Upgrading your MOS is about unrooting the weeds, which involves three steps – recognising your default settings, plugging in new beliefs to replace the old, and adopting a set of new practices to ensure your system remains up to date.

STEP 1: RECOGNISE YOUR DEFAULT SETTINGS

The first step in upgrading your MOS is to recognise your default settings.

You need to become aware of where your mind goes and what and how you're thinking – all day, every day. Then you need to recognise how these thoughts are unhelpful and replace them with better thoughts.

Here are some tools to help you do that.

Tool 1: Catch your self-talk

We talk to ourselves all the time! That inner voice can be loud or subtle, but it is there, and it is influenced by deeply engraved beliefs and biases. That voice can also help or hinder us. Let me explain...

In my case, as a person who has made a living from speaking, there has always been a tiny voice in me that says, right before a workshop starts, 'Are you sure? You don't speak English as a native. Don't make a fool of yourself!'

Then, another voice arises and says, 'You have everything you need inside of you; just be you!'

If I give in to the first voice, my mind will try to search for what might be the best way to pronounce a word or phrase, and ten times out of ten I will stumble. However, when I listen to the second voice, I tell the students upfront, 'Stop me if my accent impacts your comprehension. Otherwise, pay attention to the message!' Well, I have never been stopped by the audience due to my accent, and ten times out of ten, my mind and heart work magic and the session becomes a transformational time for both my students and me.

While it is natural for us to talk to ourselves in the mind, how-ever, it is not natural for us to catch this self-talk as it's happening. And we need to do that if we're going to improve ourselves.

If you have never paid attention to your self-talk, keeping a journal can be quite useful. This is what you can do to practise listening to yourself throughout the day:

- Allow quietness in your busy schedule to listen to your self-talk.

- Pay attention to the conversations that happen between your ears during that time. Don't get caught up in the conversation – just listen to it as an observer.
- Pull your notepad out and write your thoughts down. No need to question or argue with them. Just transfer the thoughts in your mind to paper so that your eyes can see them.
- Notice not just what you are telling yourself, but also how you talk to yourself: the tone, the emotions behind it, or even the facial expressions or gestures that might come with it.

The more you practise listening to yourself, the easier it will become. Very soon, you may notice that you can listen to yourself any time throughout the day – when you're driving, walking, waiting in line, and even when you're talking.

When you write your thoughts down, you will be able to see whether they reflect any of the default settings listed earlier – are you displaying evidence of a scarcity mindset by worrying that you don't have the resources to carry out a big project, for example? Or are you using a lot of words like 'never' and 'always' that express all-or-nothing thinking?

I used to have two big glass jars on the table in the living room, and every time a thought clearly presented itself, I wrote it down. If the thought made me feel good and happy or open and expanded, I put the piece of paper in the jar with a green tag. If the thought made me feel contracted and restricted, it went into the jar with a black tag.

Then, every month or two, I would pick a day when my mood was good and when sunlight was streaming into the room to open the jars and read the notes. I would make myself a cup of tea and spend a couple of hours reading all the notes. I would chuck out some, debate with some, and keep those that brought a smile to my face.

You can use a jar or not – it's your choice. But capturing your thoughts and writing them down is non-negotiable.

Tool 2: Reverse-engineer your thoughts

Your beliefs determine your thinking. You take actions based on your thinking. And – surprise, surprise – your actions determine your results!

So, your beliefs are important because they ultimately lead to results, but it can be really hard to find out what your beliefs are by thinking about them because your analytical brain can mislead you.

If you pay close attention, you may notice that sometimes your mind speaks to you in a very limiting way, such as:

- I'm bad with numbers/people/marketing.
- I don't have time for that fluffy stuff.
- I can't trust others.
- I need to do it, or it won't get done properly.
- I can't speak English without an accent (that's one of mine!).

All these thoughts are lies that your brain tells you, and we call them 'limiting beliefs'.

Most of the time, these thoughts come to us 'naturally'. We don't even notice that we have them, let alone know how to change them. But what you can do is reverse-engineer this sort of thinking – the belief, thought, action, results process – and start by looking at your results.

It works like this:

- Look at your results and identify what actions you took or did not take.
- Based on the actions, recognise what 'thinking' led to them.
- Based on the awareness of your 'thinking', you will become more aware of your limiting beliefs.

The point is, if you cannot catch your self-talk, look at the results you got and do a backward trace to identify how you got to where you are. Are the beliefs you discover through this process expressing any of the default settings described earlier?

STEP 2: PLUG IN NEW BELIEFS

If you use the tools described earlier, you will become aware of your limiting beliefs. As you already know, beliefs are the software of your MOS. So how do we then upgrade that software? Getting rid of the useless beliefs we acquired in the past is important, but it's equally important that we plug in new and useful beliefs.

Let's look at the beliefs you could plug in to replace the outdated and harmful ones.

Belief 1: You will never be tested beyond your capacity

We often doubt our own ability. I've met many business leaders who have great intentions and unimaginable potential, but keep talking themselves down. It's as if the ideas that make their eyes bright and their heart sing are 'just my crazy and wild thoughts' and should stay that way. But they only think this because they cannot see clearly how to execute and actualise those ideas.

I was once one of those people. Growing up in a family that

believed constant criticism is necessary for improvement, I had no confidence in myself. By default, the common pattern of thinking I developed when it came to challenges and difficulties was: 'I will fail; I am not competent enough to achieve what I desire.' Because I carried these thoughts, the behaviour I tended to display was to hide and make myself invisible so that I didn't attract any attention or judgement. I kept my hand down when I wanted to raise it, I did nothing despite wanting to push the envelope, I forced myself to stay quiet even when I wanted to stand out from the crowd ... which in turn seemed to confirm that I was incapable, incompetent and not good enough to do what I wanted to do.

But living a small, limited and constrained life is rarely our purpose. We are meant to grow and expand from our experiences. I first heard the phrase 'You will never be tested beyond your capacity' from my spiritual teacher in my early twenties. It came into my life when my heart was in a never-ending battle with my mind. What my heart desired, my mind analysed as impossible. 'Too risky!' it said. 'You don't have the experience or knowledge, and you are not competent enough to do it.'

We have learnt that it is natural for the mind to stop us from experiencing new things, because its role is to protect us and ensure we survive. So, anything new or different from what we have done or experienced in the past is considered risky and dangerous. The smarter the mind is, the more hurdles it puts in place to make sure we back off!

So, when I first heard this phrase, I was immediately lit up. Just like a strong beam of sunlight shining through dark clouds before sunrise, all the limits put in place by my intellectual mind disappeared.

You can find similar expressions in many religions, such as Christianity and Bahai faith.

Please don't disregard this idea because you don't practise a religion or trust in God. As you already know, belief is what we choose to believe is true. If we believe that we will never be tested beyond our capacity, phrases like 'This is too hard!' and 'I cannot do this,' won't be part of your language and, most importantly, won't be part of your self-talk.

We create our own reality. The moment we start to believe that we will never be tested beyond our capacity, we are open to face the fear and do it anyway. This belief changes our relationship with fear, worries and anxiety when facing uncertainty and the unknown, which are the tools used by the ego to protect us from being hurt. The job of ego is to protect our self-worth, self-image and self-concept, so it discourages us from taking risks that may lead to hurtful feelings, such as blame, shame or embarrassment. The simplest way to tame the ego is to replace the belief 'I'm the best, I should know it all' with the new belief 'I will never be tested beyond my capacity'. This buys us the opportunity to re-orient our focus from what is unknown and uncertain to what's within our control – what we can do here and now, and the possibilities and potentials that we now have the chance to bring out.

Running a business is challenging and full of unexpected lessons. We have to learn and adapt constantly. Before the new way of thinking and doing becomes our second nature, we might think it is just too hard. And it is hard, because we are in the process of building brand-new neuropathways, but this is the process of learning. I just hope that you will give it a go!

Belief 2: Only the best things will ever happen to you

'How could that be possible?!' I hear you say.

But this is a belief, and a belief is not necessarily evidence based.

You choose to believe it is true, right? So, bear with me.

Many things happen to us, both good and bad. For survival purposes, we tend to focus on and remember the 'badness' four times more than the 'goodness'. Focusing on the bad might prevent us from getting hurt next time by being extra alert and vigilant, but would it help us to handle the 'badness' better?

Avoiding is rarely the path to growth. Avoiding will never eliminate the 'bad' things that happen to us. However, if we can turn the 'bad' thing into a 'good' thing, wouldn't we grow some mental muscles in the process?

Most breakthrough moments look just like a breakdown. And this belief changes our perception of, and relationship with, difficulties and adversity; it shifts our focus from ruminating on what didn't go as well as expected and helps us to discover the benefits of this 'bad' experience.

Instead of becoming bitter or feeling sorry for ourselves, we can choose to view adversity as a pre-defined best experience. When your brain is primed in such a way, it is set up to search for the evidence that supports such beliefs. Your brain is at your service.

So, when you are experiencing hardship, pause and ask yourself:

'If only the best things can happen to me, what about this experience could be the "BEST" now, or in five or ten years?'

'Am I getting more clarity and strengthening my character in the midst of this adversity?'

'What can I gain from this experience that would benefit me in the long term?'

'Am I gaining specific new skills, new knowledge or new tools from this experience?'

When adversity is an adversity, we struggle and feel frustrated. Those feelings are usually an indicator that the skills and knowledge we have are not sufficient to deal with the challenge we are facing. In the process of surviving the adversity, we may gain some new knowledge, acquire some new tools from the discomfort, and rethink what we truly want to be successful.

I often applaud people who experience their share of hardship in their younger years. Having a smooth trip to success in your twenties or thirties is not necessarily a good thing. Let's be honest. Regardless of how smart or fortunate you are, there are life lessons you have to learn. If we stumble and fall, those lessons come to us earlier.

Have you ever experienced the collapse of a belief system? If you have, you would understand my feelings when everything I believed in, everything I thought I knew, everything I had worked hard for since high school, was flipped upside down when I was twenty-two.

It took me almost ten years to get healed, to rebuild my confidence, and at the same time learn new knowledge and skills to pull me out of the rut. It was dark in that rut, and most of the time I felt frustrated and helpless, like I was trying to find a track that no one I knew had walked before.

For a very long time, I thought those years were the darkest time of my life, and I refused to mention it to anyone. Then, after ten years, right in the middle of a workshop I was conducting, when I was explaining the concept of intrinsic motivation, I suddenly realised the meaning of that experience. Without it, I wouldn't have been able to change my career from practising law and fighting for right or wrong, to practising actualising human potentials and fighting for what could be possible. I wouldn't have been able to do what I was meant to do in this life.

If you can harness your mind to explore the questions listed earlier, you will quickly move away from a fixed mindset to a growth mindset. This will release frustration, refocus your energy on what you can do now, and give you the confidence that you will be better off by owning everything that you experience.

Kintsugi, an ancient practice that was born in Japan in the 1500s, is the art of repairing broken pottery by joining the pieces with gold to highlight imperfections instead of hiding them. This makes the repaired pottery more unique and valuable. We are that pottery – the final version of us that experienced hardship and adversities holds great beauty and value.

If you are walking in your darkness now, be patient, and curious.

Belief 3: Your mind is not always right

Before taking time to know our minds intimately, we tend to think that every single thought that pops up is the absolute truth. But they are NOT! Thoughts are just thoughts; they are NOT absolute truth. There is no need to believe in everything your mind says or even take it seriously, so don't treat it as the one and only reliable source of information for your decision making.

The role our mind plays is to filter, distort and ignore information, and make things up so that we stick with what we already know – what's familiar and safe – and see what we want to see. Once you know this to be true, you are able to also listen to your gut feelings and tap into your intuition. This gives us access to information that doesn't register on a conscious level.

Our formal education tends to keep us in our heads all the time, and present ourselves as rational and logical beings. But this is not true. Humans are emotional beings. We will discuss this more in the following chapters. But for now, give yourself the permission to NOT just believe what your mind tells you.

However, to achieve your greatness, you must conquer your mind! Notice your thought, give it the attention it needs, no more and no less, don't hold it tightly, and don't spin with it. You need to listen to your mind, gut and heart. When these three elements are combined, you will know the truth.

STEP 3: EMPLOY NEW PRACTICES

To be successful is not about what you know, or what you do. It is about what you do consistently on a regular basis, which we call habitual practices. Let's now look at the practices that you can adopt that will upgrade your MOS and therefore upgrade your results.

Practice 1: Challenge and be flexible with your thinking

Previously, we talked about catching your self-talk by listening to and writing down your inner conversations. Writing is a great way to understand ourselves, as it allows us to reveal the hidden patterns in our subconscious. But now we need to take this much further. I want you to not only capture your thoughts, but then assess them, challenge them and re-write them in a more constructive and realistic way. This will help you make permanent changes to your distorted and unhelpful thinking patterns – patterns that ultimately lead to undesirable behaviour.

Step 1: Capture your thoughts

Recording your thoughts will help you get clear on what your thinking is. But you need to do more than just dabble in this. If you dabble, you won't make progress, because capturing and recording thoughts requires discipline, courage and persistence.

So we're going to take this a step further by creating a 'Thoughts Log', which looks like this:

Situation (What happened)	I was asked to give a keynote in my second language at an industrial event, and I felt quite anxious so I said 'No'.
Your thoughts (What you're thinking about)	It is impossible, I speak English with an accent, I will make a fool of myself.
Underlying core values (What drives the thoughts)	Perfection.
Underlying beliefs (What contributes to the values)	Only people who speak with no accent should give keynotes.

As a novice thought recorder, you may notice that it is kind of challenging to separate your thoughts, your feelings and the underlying values and beliefs. This is quite normal, so don't be discouraged, but keep logging more thoughts. The more you practise, the more clarity you will get. Just like any other skill, practise make perfect, and you don't need perfection here – you need persistence and clarity.

Step 2: Assess your thoughts

The second practice that will help you upgrade your MOS is to use the ladder of inference to break down the thought process. Let's continue with the example above of 'Saying NO to giving a keynote in a second language.' If we start from the bottom of the ladder of inference, it would look like this:

Rung 1 (Reality and Facts): I was asked to give a keynote in English, my second language.

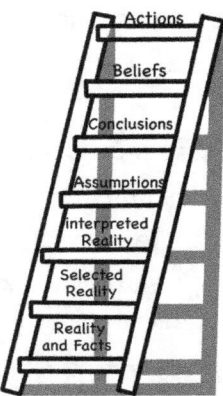

Rung 2 (Selected Reality): English is my second language, and I have an accent.

Rung 3 (Interpreted Reality): I don't speak as well as native speakers, so I will be judged and criticised and laughed at.

Rung 4 (Assumptions): When I don't speak perfectly, people will laugh at me and perceive me as incompetent.

Rung 5 (Conclusions): I will make a fool of myself.

Rung 6 (Beliefs): Only people who speak with no accent should give keynotes.

Rung 7 (Actions): Reject the offer, saying 'No'.

After laying out all your thoughts on paper, the fun starts! You can now argue with them, ask questions or debate with them – do all you need to put things in perspective.

For example, at Rung 2, my attention was focused on the selected reality of 'my accent', and I completely ignored other facts, such as:

- The organiser is not an idiot! He won't ask a person who is incapable of speaking to speak at his event.
- Even if I do have an accent, people who have been through my training or workshops have never complained that they couldn't understand me.

At Rung 3, I interpreted the situation according to the biases of my selected reality, which led me to the assumptions, conclusions and beliefs of the next three rungs. At Rung 6, did you see a limiting belief there? Gosh, do I really think that people with an accent should not give keynotes?? These days, I can easily argue with these assumptions, conclusions and beliefs by asking a few simple questions.

Some of those questions include:

- What is the evidence that your competence will be judged due to your accent? When and where did this happen before and who was involved?
- If you are incompetent due to your accent, why do people keep asking you to present?
- Is it true that someone can truly speak with no accent at all?
- Honestly, who doesn't speak with an accent? Accent can be part of the personality, right?
- Has anyone considered you a fool because of your accent? Who? When?
- What else do people seek to gain from your keynote, besides your accent?
- Is there anything good about this situation?
- Will this matter in five years' time?

Arguing with the mind is fun. All you need to do is NOT take your thoughts as absolute truth. Because they are not!

If you can, spend time digging deeper to understand where this thought comes from. And give your final assessment: is it still useful today? Once you've done that, you can add two more rows to the Thoughts Log, as I have done here:

Situation (What happened)	I was asked to give a keynote in my second language at an industrial event, and I felt quite anxious so I said 'No'.
Your thoughts (What I'm thinking about)	It is impossible, I don't speak English as well as native speakers, I will make a fool of myself.
Underlying core values (What drives the thoughts)	Perfection.
Underlying beliefs (What contributes to the values)	Only people who speak with no accent should give keynotes.
Where did they (values and beliefs) come from?	Parents tend to be critical, gave me no praise at home, only high standards to meet. They did so with good intentions, but it hurts my confidence.
Are they still useful today?	No.

When you have all the answers, you can move to the next step.

Step 3: Re-write your thoughts

Re-writing thoughts is the most important part of the process of re-wiring your mind.

In neuroscience there is a concept called 'neuroplasticity'. Basically, it means your brain is malleable even as an adult, and both the structure and function of your brain can change according to what you pay attention to, how you interpret your experiences and what you focus on.

Canadian neuroscientist Donald Hebb, the father of neuropsy-chology, famously explained the dilemma with what is now known as the Hebbian theory, which was coined by Carla Shatz, the first woman to receive a PhD in neurobiology from Harvard and now head of the University's Department of Neurobiology. The Hebbian theory asserts that:

'Neurons (cells) that fire together wire together.'

In layman's terms, this means that when brain cells are simul-taneously activated, the synaptic strength between those cells increases. This creates a strong connection between these cells, which eventually become neuropathways. Consequently, this results in loss of connection between other cells.

This ability to create neuropathways is important, as it helps us make sense of the more than four billion bits of information that we have to filter every second so that we only pay attention to what is important.

It also means that when those neuropathways are unhelpful, we can take steps to change them by taking advantage of the brain's neuroplasticity. To do this we need to be intentional. Being intentional is about being clear about the results you want. When you set an intention to achieve a specific outcome or result that is important to you, your mind and body work together to help you.

Remember, your mind is at your service. When you take back ownership, prime it and give it the right instructions, it is set up to work *for* you, not *against* you. Re-writing your thoughts with intention gives them the power to lead us down a path of success.

Thinking intentionally means taking back control of our thoughts and reactions. It means being present with our thoughts and choosing them with awareness. Each thought you have should enable you to focus on what's really important to you. This allows us to get the best out of our thoughts and can shift us from the passenger seat, where we get carried away by our thoughts, to the driver's seat, where we are in control of where we are heading.

The only thing that we can have complete control over is our thinking, so being intentional with our thoughts holds great power.

Now let's look at how this works in practice by continuing with the example of my fear of keynote speaking:

Situation (**What happened**)	I was asked to give a keynote in my second language at an industrial event, and I felt quite anxious so I said 'No'.
Your thoughts (**What I'm thinking about**)	It is impossible, I don't speak English as well as native speakers, I will make a fool of myself.
Underlying core values (**What drives the thoughts**)	Perfection.
Underlying beliefs (**What contributes to the values**)	Only people who speak with no accent should give keynotes.
Where did they (values and beliefs) come from?	Parents tend to be critical, gave me no praise at home, only high standards to meet. They did so with good intentions, but it hurts my confidence.
Are they still useful today?	No.
The NEW and useful belief for this situation	*When I speak from the heart, my accent won't stop me from making connections with the audience.* *Connection is more important than accent.*

Given the relationship between your thoughts and actions, and the results this process delivers, each thought should serve a particular purpose that is relevant to the result desired. Question yourself and explicitly spell out the relationships between your thoughts and outcomes.

The more clearly you can see the relationship between thoughts and actions, the clearer your thoughts become.

Practice 2: Expand your mind by designing your environment

Humans are adaptive for survival purposes. Our environment shapes us as a person. So expanding your mind starts from designing your environment.

Your environment includes more than just your physical environment. It also includes the people you spend time with, the conversations you have, the books you read, the podcasts you listen to, and the inspirations you are exposed to. You've probably heard the quote, most often attributed to motivational speaker Jim Rohn: 'You are the product of the five people that you surround yourself with.'

We have control over our own internal environment, and we also have control over what or who is allowed to influence it. If we do not take control of that consistently by being selective about what we allow into our minds, we will spend a lot of the time fixing it and feeling like we're a victim of circumstances.

But we are not victims of anything but ourselves; to the image we hold of ourselves; to the standards we set for ourselves; and to the discipline and desire we have to create something different for ourselves.

....

Without doubt the most common weakness of all human beings is the habit of leaving their minds open to the negative influence of other people.

— NAPOLEON HILL

....

What are you giving your focused attention to right now and is it serving you? Who and what are you allowing to influence your mind right now and is it serving you?

If you are a busy business leader, designing your environment also means taking personal responsibility for being aware of what's in your environment and choosing what goes into your mind. For example:

- Note what you **watch or read**. What you watch and read gets into your subconscious, so choose wisely.
- Pay attention to **where** you are spending your time outside the office. The activities you're involved in either lift you up and expand you mind, or push you deeper into your comfort zone.
- Evaluate **who** you are spending time with. If you surround yourself with people who ONLY agree with you, you are paving the way to failure. Instead, find people whose minds are more advanced than yours, who are capable of asking provoking questions, who view things differently and who are brave enough to share their perspectives with you.

Designing an environment for mind expansion requires you to break away from old, unhelpful comforts. The more you can disrupt the norm, the better.

Practice 3: Safeguard your attention

Attention is our most precious commodity these days.

Paying attention to something keeps everything else in the shadows. Imagine your attention is a torch, and when you point it towards something it lights up a small area with its focused beams so that you can see the object clearly. But outside of that focused beam, everything is absorbed by darkness – you cannot see what is in the darkness unless you redirect the torch.

We make choices and take actions according to what and where we pay attention to. To be a productive thinker, and hence a productive leader, you can practise safeguarding your attention so that it can be allocated to what matters. Let's look at a few ways to do that.

Mute distractions

When trying to maintain focus it can be difficult to ignore distractions. Studies have shown that constant distraction can disrupt our concentration and reduce our ability to focus on the tasks at hand. The more you can reduce distractions while you are working, the more productive you will be in the long run.

Eliminating possible distractions can be done by establishing clear boundaries and rules for work, avoiding any type of communication that is not essential, and using tools that reduce the likelihood of interruptions. For example, eliminating all non-essential forms of communication while you are working. This includes things like checking social media, responding to emails, or chatting to team members randomly. Or, you can use tools that are specifically designed to minimise distractions. These include programs, such as **Friday Planner** or **Freedom**, that block websites that are known sources of distraction, and applications that will automatically reply to your emails for you so that you don't have to deal with them while you are working.

Stop multi-tasking

Multi-tasking doesn't make you smart. In fact, the more you do it, the more stupid you get! Research suggests that multi-tasking lowers your IQ score by ten to fifteen points.[2] Even worse, a study conducted in 2012 by York University showed that students who were multi-tasking on their laptops during a lecture scored eleven per cent lower than non-multi-taskers in a comprehension test. Even the people sitting next to them underperformed in the test.[3]

When we multi-task, the brain is constantly 'switching' – jumping back and forth from task A to task B. The brain consumes more than twenty per cent of the energy produced by the body when it's idle, so 'switching' and 'jumping' consumes even more energy and makes you get tired easily. And when your brain is tired, what happens? Mistakes!

Research published in 2010 claimed that only 2.5 per cent of people can multi-task effectively.[4] Who might they be? Surgeons are one type, conference interpreters another. Have you ever experienced simultaneous interpreting at a conference? This is when, regardless of the languages the speakers present in, you can hear what they say in your choice of language through your earphones.

These interpreters are trained to listen-translate-speak simultaneously. When I was a student learning linguistics, I tried it once or twice. During the conference we sat in a booth with a partner, and each of us translated for thirty minutes, then took a rest for thirty minutes, then translated again for thirty minutes. To this day, I still remember putting my head into cold water afterwards and steam coming out. My brain was burning!

For most of us, the more we multi-task, the less we accomplish! So stop multi-tasking and focus on one thing at a time. Here are some tips to help you do that:

- Keep just one window open on your computer.
- Turn off notifications on your phone and computer.
- Notice the thoughts that come into your mind, park them, and attend to them later.
- Do one thing – the thing requires your cognitive ability – at a time!

Reset your attention in nature

In 2008, a study was conducted to find a better way to regain attention and focus for improved performance.[5] Participants were bombarded by stimuli (honking cars, billboards, people talking), which taxed their attention, and they had to decide which of the stimuli to pay attention to and which to ignore. The longer we stay in such an environment, the more we suffer Directed Attentional Fatigue (DAF), a term used in psychology that describes the impaired ability to concentrate or pay attention which, inevitably, will impact our mental performance negatively.

The human brain has an 'inhibitory attention system' that enables us to pay attention to certain things while ignoring other stimuli, which helps us to stay focused despite external and internal distractions. This is why some people can sit in a crowded café and work on their laptops, or work or read on busy subways, or keep worries and concerns about future events in the back of their mind.

However, when this inhibitory system is overworked, we may start to feel irritated and become impatient with the things that usually don't bother us.

According to Stephen and Rachel Kaplan's Attention Restoration Theory, you can reset your attention in nature, which means scheduling time to escape into nature. Even spending just twenty minutes in nature can help to relieve your mental fatigue and restore your ability to focus and concentrate. You can find nature in your backyard or in parks that you have access to. Wherever you go, make it a priority to escape from your daily hassles and into greenery!

Practise meditation

Meditation is about brain training and is an umbrella name given to all kinds of brain training, such as mindfulness, body scanning and transcendental meditation. All these are brain training techniques that target various areas of the brain.

In the past few decades, the amount of research on meditation has exploded. Our mind is busy all the time. It works 24/7 and thoughts constantly appear in the mind. Without deliberate practice, it is quite normal to become trapped on the wheel of whirling thoughts and get carried away by the feelings and emotions attached to those thoughts. Research shows that by practising meditation on a regular basis, focus and memory will be improved and stress and anxiety are better managed.[6][7] Basically, meditation provides a calm mind that makes it possible to see our thoughts clearly as they arise.

In the book *Altered Traits*, Daniel Goleman and Richard Davidson share their decades of cutting-edge research on meditation, such as the surprising changes made in the structure of the brain and, consequently, personality traits.

If meditation is not part of your daily routine yet, start now with three minutes three times a day. When you work on quieting down your mind, you may hear more of what's happening inside it. Look for **Headspace, Calmer**, **Waking Up** and **Insight Timer** in the App Store – all provide rich resources to get you started on this practice.

What's next?

*A lack of clarity could put the brakes
on any journey to success.*

STEVE MARABOLI

The mental operating system we use will either create problems for us or solve them. Constantly and persistently upgrading our MOS will enable us to gain **clarity**.

As business leaders, living successfully means living intentionally, which requires clarity. Clarity makes everything easier; it helps you to see what matters, what needs to be changed and what you need to focus on.

When your thinking is muddied by distortions, distractions and self-limiting beliefs, achieving goals becomes an ever more daunting 'mission impossible'. But when you spend time on understanding how your mind works and identifying its default settings, you will be able to remove hidden, self-made obstacles in the form of limiting beliefs and distorted thinking patterns. You will stop wasting time on overthinking and instead find your focus and direction. You will push through doubt.

The more clarity you get, the more you can distinguish between the voices inside you and choose wisely which to listen to.

Here's a simple self-assessment to understand the current state of your MOS.

Self-assessment: Mental Operating System

The scale for each statement is 1–5.
1 = the statement does NOT resonate with me at all
5 = the statement describes exactly the way things are in my life

	1	2	3	4	5
1. I'm good at prioritising my time and tasks.					
2. I'm good at setting goals and achieving them.					
3. I'm good at focusing on what matters.					
4. I'm good at gaining perspectives and reaching decisions.					
5. I'm good at keeping my commitment.					
6. I'm good at blocking out distractions.					
7. I'm good at thinking critically and creatively.					

My score is: _____

Chapter 2

Spiritual Operating System

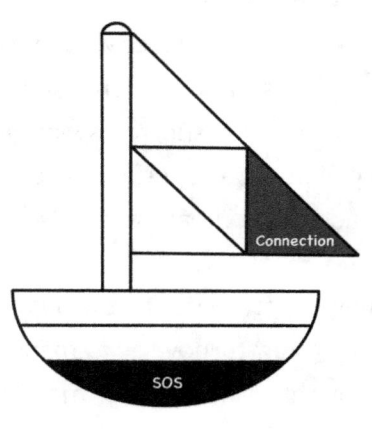

When we are spiritually healthy, we realise that we
exist beyond the physical and our life has a sense of
meaning and purpose.

— ROBYN L. GOBIN

Mark is the CEO of an innovative services business. He
started the business from his garage, and slowly built it into
a national name with several hundred employees across
all states.

Five years ago, he started to extend his business into
the relevant industry and recruited a group of bright and

hard-working professionals to quickly gain market awareness.

Getting to where he is today was not easy. He experienced tremendous setbacks but, bit by bit, he built his business into a success story. He believes the reason he was able to do this is because he surrounded himself with capable people whose priority was to support his dream and ambitions ONLY. So, questions were not welcomed, different opinions or perspectives were not welcomed, mistakes were not welcomed. But putting a spin on things was considered smart, playing in the grey area was brave, taking shortcuts was wise, and solving customer complaints on a superficial level was acceptable! None of this made the company a very welcoming place to work.

Unfortunately, twenty years into the business, Mark began to experience high staff turnover – as many as 200 resignations in a month. This high turnover meant that Mark was constantly searching for employees, most of whom didn't stay for more than six months. He thought it was because he is not good at 'people stuff', so he continued to pay a huge marketing firm to manage his 'image'. If he met you at your desk, he regarded it as a photo opportunity. If he gave you a birthday present, there would have to be a photo ... and all these photos were posted publicly to create the idea that his company was a 'wonderful place to work'.

When I first met Mark, he was puzzled. He had gained awards in his industry, but at the same time he was closely watched by the spectators in the industry. He was portrayed as a warm, caring and happy leader in public, but in private, he rarely smiled.

'What's wrong?' he asked.

Meet your soul

'Soul' is not a term that we often use in the business world, but we do sometimes hear comments like: 'This business has a soul!' or 'We put our heart and soul into this project.'

The soul is in charge of our spiritual operating system (**SOS**). But what is the soul?

A dictionary definition of the soul is:

1. *The spiritual or immaterial part of a human being or animal, regarded as immortal.*
2. *Emotional or intellectual energy or intensity, especially as revealed in a work of art or an artistic performance.'*

The soul has been a subject of study since the time of Socrates. Scientists, philosophers and religious leaders have long been curious about the soul's shape and location, and have searched for evidence of its existence. When I became interested in psychology, one of the first textbooks I opened said: 'Psychology means study of soul.' Hallelujah! And while I've never been concerned about what my soul looks like or where it lives, what truly intrigues me is WHAT does it DO?

The soul is in charge of your values, character, purpose and meaning. Its role is to create challenges, difficulties and obstacles for us by putting speed bumps on our path, which force us to slow down, observe, reflect and change gears, and choose what to do in those moments. It is only in those moments that who we truly are gets the chance to show up, and who we truly are is a combination of our values, character, purpose and meaning.

Your values are the things that you believe are important in the way you live and work. They are established throughout your life through the accumulation of experiences, they tend to be relatively stable, and they represent the outward manifestation of your character.

Your values affect the decisions you make, how you perceive your environment and how you behave. Basically, values are fundamental ideas and beliefs that guide you (or your company's) motivations and decisions, such as honesty, transparency and helpfulness.

Your character is an amalgamation of your qualities and characteristics, which makes you unique and helps you stand apart from the rest. In the business world, character is everything! It is evidenced by what you do when you have nothing to gain. Good character doesn't just build the trust needed for success. It helps you perform your role in connecting, engaging and motivating your people as a leader. In my line of work, there is a popular saying: hire on character and develop skills. In Mark's case, people were leaving the business due to the character of the big boss, who was effectively making a living by leading a dual life. He liked to portray himself as a warm, caring boss who was close to his employees and fun to work with, but when the camera was off all the smiles were gone.

Purpose and meaning are the drivers of our actions. What we do and say, or what we don't do and say, or how we do and say things, all serve some purpose and have some meaning. But so many of us are unconscious of our behaviours, the language we use, the decisions we make and the actions we take. We say things without really knowing why we're saying it, and we do things without clearly knowing the purpose or ripple effects of our actions. When we are unconscious to these things, we will surely experience more speed bumps and repeatedly run into similar situations until we learn the lesson and get clearer about the purpose and meaning of our existence.

Realising these facts can be a spiritual awakening for many, and it might not be the path we would take through life and work if we had a choice. Because it is a path that involves diligent and courageous inner work to search the soul, to have a dialogue with it, to see the connections between the events we experience, and find the meaning of why and how.

HOW YOUR SOS WORKS

Being spiritual involves the recognition of a feeling or sense or belief that there is something greater than ourselves, which provides us with a sense of meaning, purpose and connectedness. When we see ourselves as part of the greater whole, we inevitably ponder what our role is in this greater whole – are we consuming and burdening the greater whole, or are we contributing to and nurturing it?

When you get in touch with your spiritual self, you get pumped up with energy that makes you optimistic and courageous. In times of adversity, you are able to keep calm. You accept and forgive more easily, and you rebound and re-orient your focus on what matters more quickly. In essence, you can see the forest as well as the trees more clearly, and you are able to connect the dots. When Mark said he was not happy, his unhappiness was rooted in WHY and HOW he did what he did, not just WHAT he did.

You don't need to believe in God or convert to any religion to have your spiritual operating system up and running, although religion could be a good place to gain spiritual education. But you do need to seek a meaningful connection with something bigger than yourself. And it helps you to recognise that your role in life has a greater value than what you do every day.

As a business leader, when your SOS runs smoothly, it has the power and capability to release you from the rat race that has trapped so many people. It can help you find confidence and certainty in the middle of chaos, and experience positive emotions like peace, gratitude and acceptance in the face of adversity.

Your SOS works chiefly by putting you in situations that you must draw lessons from. You will find that questions are posed, such as:

- What gives my life meaning and purpose?
- What gives me hope?
- How do I get through tough times? Where do I find comfort?
- Do my values guide my decisions and actions?
- Am I fulfilling my roles, responsibilities and missions here?

These questions help you to better understand your inner life, so that you act more wisely in the outer world.

As Socrates said: 'Know thyself.' This is the one and only mission we carry in this life. We come to know ourselves through interacting with others and via the ups and downs on our journey, through which we discover why we care about what we care about and why we do what we do the way we do it. We know ourselves better through the experiences we have.

Spirituality enables us to gain a clearer understanding of life, of how things work, of how things are connected. It allows us to see the bigger picture and recognise our roles in the context of the greater reality. This phenomenon can only be experienced. You can read about it, listen to stories about it, but it will do nothing for you until you have waded the waters and actually experienced it.

DEFAULT SETTINGS OF THE SOS

Just as a machine comes out of the factory with certain default settings, our spiritual operating system also came with default settings.

Let's look at common default settings of the SOS in the business world:

Powered down

I often hear people comment that 'Spirituality is for weak people. Only those who have lots of problems in life or do not have the strength to face life need the support of the concept of a higher power.'

Aha!

Why do people who have problems come to spirituality?

Because that is how most of the human race seems to work. Only in adversity or total desperation do we tend to ask meaningful questions about our existence. In happy times, most of us act like we are going to live forever with everything and everyone we love around us. Our wealth, family and everything that matters to us ... will remain the same for eternity.

I am no different. I went through my darkest time right after university, which made me question a lot of things that I took for granted. By crawling out of that darkness, I developed a thirst for knowing more about the world and I very naturally gravitated towards spirituality. To this day, I am thankful for that 'unfortunate' episode in my life.

So, if you think being spiritual means you are weak, think of some of those people whose spirituality gave them incredible power: Mahatma Gandhi, Martin Luther King Jr, Mother Teresa ... the list goes on. Not only were these people strong enough to create profound change in the lives of other people – they gained that strength from their spirituality. In other words, their SOS was operating at full capacity.

People who have a deep understanding of their own spiritual self are invariably strong, stable and compassionate. A person's strength, stability and compassion are the best measures of how deeply they understand their spirituality.

Intellectualised

When we try to describe spirituality intellectually, we often fail. It's hard to find the words to describe what it's like to have a spiritual experience to someone who has never had one. Most of us have logic as our default setting when it comes to spiritual matters. Our logical mind works to ensure:

- We only trust what we see. If we can't see it, it doesn't exist.
- We categorise all things as good or bad, right or wrong.
- We attribute good fortune to our personal greatness and blame others or the circumstances for our misfortune.
- We micromanage ourselves, so that everything is planned and nothing unexpected happens.

We also put aside questions that our logical mind cannot answer, such as:

- Who we are?
- What is the purpose or meaning of life?
- Why do we experience what we experience?

Answering these questions is not comfortable for us if our SOS has its logic settings too high. We think that people who spend time on figuring these things out are weirdos, and no one likes to be seen as a weirdo. So we focus on the shallow stuff in life, the material things, the money, the status ... turning our head away and doing what others do and competing as others do. Or we might just try to intellectualise spiritual practices.

I have often met people who say, 'I have read so many books about meditation, and I've heard so many stories about its bene-fits, but I still can't control my anger, so I don't think this works for me.' Like any spiritual practice, meditation won't benefit us if we just understand the theory. It requires practice – consistent and persistent practice – so that we can internalise the theory, create our own stories and experience the benefits. But too many of us tend to learn everything with our intellectual mind ONLY, and avoid the practice, which leads to faking it!

Superficial

Some people may think their spirituality is functioning well, but in fact their default setting is 'superficial'. When 'spirituality' as a topic comes up in conversation, these people start to share about how so and so went to India or Tibet for a spiritual retreat; or so and so is wearing this priceless necklace or bracelet that is blessed by a guru; or so and so donated so much so that they are well protected from illness, unhappiness and misfortune; or so and so is so spiritual that he/she cares so little about material things that he/she feels comfortable to live on social welfare...

Honestly, hearing these things makes me question their under-standing of spirituality! Let me explain...

It is true that when your SOS is upgraded, you may choose to conduct yourself differently. For example, you may choose to consume the products that add less burden to the Earth, you may wish to surround yourself with people who are walking on a similar path, and you may also re-assess the value of many things that were once important to you. However, when you make these changes, they should happen from the inside out – not the other way around.

It is true that when our SOS is well upgraded, we do not overly attach ourselves to material stuff, and gain more joy and reward from non-material things. But using 'spirituality' to avoid respon-sibility when we are capable of contributing to society, or taking advantage of the social welfare system when we don't need to, is totally wrong!

It is true that seeing the connections between events allows us to be more accepting and not cling to or crave what is tempo-rary, but twisting this into a justification for not taking personal responsibilities is totally wrong!

It is true that growing your spirituality allows you to access more positive emotions, like awe, joy and contentment, but repressing unpleasant feelings, or judging yourself or others for expressing strong emotions like anger or sadness when necessary, is totally wrong!

It is also true that having our spirituality awakened by practising meditation or yoga, or praying or serving in the holy lands, helps us to grow our spiritual being, but feeling superior for doing these things is totally wrong! When your 'awakened' spiritual achievements make it harder for you to tolerate others, it is time to watch your spiritual ego.

True spirituality is a lifelong inside-out practice, instead of preaching! There's a huge difference between 'knowing the path' and 'walking the path'. Simply memorising sacred scripts, and relying on our intellectual minds to understand spiritual concepts without internalising them by acting them out, may actually block us from having a deep experience of the truth and keep us stuck in the hell of dogmatic thinking.

True spirituality requires us to constantly travel into the inner world, clarify our purpose, strengthen our values, shift our beliefs and adjust our behaviours so that our unconscious choices won't burden or harm the wider system and we can make positive impact via our conduct.

Again, awakening your soul and being spiritual is about what you do for others. It is not measured by what you wear, which guru is in your picture, who you worship, or whether you swear or drink or are poor or rich. Instead, it is measured by how many lives you impacted positively, how many souls you lifted up, and how much love and support you offered.

As a business leader, when you meet your soul, chances are, you will be able to build a business that has a soul.

Egocentric

We all have egos. We can't get rid of our ego, but we can manage it. However, if our SOS is not upgraded, we may well find that our ego is untamed. A properly functioning SOS allows us to see that we are just one cog in a much greater universe, and that we are here to serve both others and ourselves. But an untamed ego seeks only to serve itself, and therefore can be harmful.

History tells us that many leaders failed miserably because of their egos. For example, Steve Jobs was kicked out of Apple because of his ego. It was the same for Mark, who we discussed earlier – he almost lost the business that he spent twenty years building because of his unmanaged ego. When he gave the cold shoulder to people who expressed different views or pointed out different perspectives, his ego took control and sent a loud, clear and company-wide message for everyone to 'Shut up and do what I say!'

Everything in business starts with you, and everything in business ends with you!

When leaders' egos are not well managed, they believe that their way is the only way. They refuse to listen to hurtful but useful criticism. They shut their employees down and keep them in the dark and in silence. While such a leader is the centre of everything at work, the culture they create is frustrating for talented employees, for whom leaving becomes the only option.

Moreover, such a leader's ego won't let them see reality, and these leaders believe they are doing the right thing for the business even when this is clearly not the case. When Mark silenced his leadership team and stopped them from expressing different views and perspectives, his ego separated him from reality. Failure became inevitable.

Ego is how we see ourselves, and is developed when we're little, when we rely on a caregiver to feed us, entertain us and protect us. Basically, the world revolves around us when we're little, so naturally ego is developed according to the distorted way we see ourselves. It protects us from reality and seeks to use any means to ensure we feel good about ourselves.

Many adults, business leaders included, haven't grown out of this egocentric state. They believe that bad things happen to them and others cause them trouble, and that they are conditioned to do what they need to do even if they might not be proud of what they did.

When ego plays the role of protector, it wants us to feel we are brilliant, smart, competent, articulate, eloquent, wise ... and perfect human beings. It is easily offended, so when our behaviours are questioned, regardless of whether we intended to make a mistake, the ego will direct us to find excuses, reasons and explanations for our failings so that we can still feel good about ourselves. Ego protects us by making us believe we are infallible and perfect.

The ego won't stop working until it is satisfied that it has painted an image in our heads that 'We are absolutely right; others are wrong.' It does this by all means and through all kinds of defensive behaviours, such as pointing our finger at others, blaming circum-stances, back-biting, telling lies or distorting reality. You name it, ego covers our insecurity and paints a portrait of ourselves as perfect beings who never make mistakes.

But the truth is, we are human beings, and to be human is to make mistakes.

Managing your ego is acknowledging that we are perfectly flawed as humans. That we make mistakes. If we can manage our ego, we can accept this and face it, which will make us humble and vulnerable. Being vulnerable enables us to be authentic and self-aware.

Managing your ego and helping it to function in a healthy manner is quite possible and very necessary for business leaders, although it does require a strong desire to know yourself, to face your shadow, and to keep going.

BENEFITS OF UPGRADING YOUR SOS

Simply put, upgrading your SOS as a business leader makes you attractive for the right reasons. You may be rich and generous, but do you want to be attractive only for your deep pockets?

Upgrading our SOS is about revealing who we truly are. About strengthening our character and integrity and our faith, and hence benefiting from the energy it brings to our life. The level of your spiritual energy is determined by your deeds and is triggered by your values.

Nowadays, more and more companies are openly talking about spirituality as an integral part of their corporate culture. In doing so, they prove that spirituality does not harm the company's success but helps it.

There is a growing body of research showing that incorporating ethics and spiritual values into the workplace can lead to increased productivity and profitability, as well as improved employee retention, customer loyalty and brand reputation. When you incorporate spirituality into your business, you transform the personality of the company from an empty shell to a living entity. Spirituality gives a company a soul.

You will be more successful

Usually, spirituality is not something we openly talk about in business settings. But there are leaders who have been open about their spiritual beliefs, and have said that they have been informed and inspired by faith and spirituality. Indra Nooyi, former CEO of PepsiCo, is one of those leaders. She believes that performance and purpose mutually reinforce each other, and that financial success is married to social responsibility.

As a leader whose spiritual operating system is strong and robust, you incorporate your beliefs and core values into all matters of your life and business. You measure success by internal features such as character, contributions and the quality of your services, more than external ones such as fame and material possessions.

You will be more self-aware, and better able to see the connections between your thinking and doing and the results, as well as the effect this has on others. You will be more mindful of your choice of words and actions, and wiser in how to influence the people you can reach. Your SOS makes you more human, and demonstrating human virtues through your work will make you a better leader, and a better leader will inevitably be more successful.

You will move beyond self-interest

If you look at the website of almost any business, you are likely to find a list of company values, sometimes even a vision and mission statement. If you were to walk around their office, you may also see posters and signs related to their values, vision and mission hanging on the walls. It's as if by putting those words down they will 'become' who they describe in those words, or at least increase the possibility that they will. For many, this is just wishful thinking. It takes deep inner work to gain such congruence.

To be fair, what we care about does evolve when we mature. When we're young, we care about what is relevant to our survival. Later, we try to fulfil the needs that revolve around personal interests, such as the size of our house, the brand of our car, our circle of supporters and followers, and the fame and name we make for ourselves in society. These are all the things that our egos want us to have so that when we compare ourselves to others, we can feel good about ourselves.

We might undertake activities that, on the surface, appear to be altruistic. For example, we may get involved in charity work or projects that are intended to benefit the greater good, but what drives us to do these things is the desire to attract attention and put ourselves in the limelight. Our activities say, 'Look at me, look at me, look how great I am!' This is the voice of your ego, and ego exists to serve your personal interest.

When I met Mark's team, I frequently heard them say, 'We just do what he wants us to do.'

'What if you have different views?' I asked.

'We are employed to do what he asks, not to think,' some joked.

'But on the wall, I saw slogans like "Care about your clients as if they are your family" and "Care about the business as if it is yours". How do you care without telling the truth?'

'Ah, those – they're just put there for visitors to see; it's not how we operate here. Mark is the founder, and we are expected to do whatever he wants us to do.'

'I did see the photos showing that you have been involved in many charity events. Is that the cause you personally support?'

> 'Ha, that is just for show!'
>
> 'How does that make you feel?'
>
> 'Don't you know how many people left the business last month?'

If you can upgrade your SOS, you will grow out of your ego-driven state. Then, chances are, you will start to see the role you play in the wider system and to care about the wellbeing of people you will never meet. You will start to pay attention to your actions and how they affect others. You're likely to start caring about people and the planet and be driven to do the right thing in the right way.

It doesn't matter whether your name is remembered; it matters that you are doing the work to serve and benefit the people you care about the most, and to solve the problems that you care about the most. Fame and attention are by-products of your actions; they are not the motivation for your actions. With or without fame and attention, you do what you are determined to do.

It doesn't matter whether your values, vision and mission are hanging on the wall of your office. It matters whether your choices and behaviours are in alignment with your values. When such alignment is in place, you and your business will attract the right people into your life – people who also care deeply about values and purpose beyond their personal interest.

HOW TO UPGRADE YOUR SOS

Upgrading your SOS is about knowing yourself MUCH more deeply! So deep that sometimes you have to hold your breath and dive deep into the water to meet your hidden self. It is not about skimming the surface and finding your favourite colour, food or music. It is about delving much deeper and discovering who you are as a human being: the real you.

Knowing self is a journey. Sometimes it is unpredictable and brings you face to face with your deepest fears, self-doubts and insecurities. It is the journey that makes you question how you are living your life and running your business, and whether it is in alignment with your highest purpose.

It is a journey that can be challenging and scary, and therefore many people would rather choose to deal with the same obstacles over and over again rather than embark on the inward journey to solve the problem at the core. Remember that 'we create our own realities'!

Be brave and curious, and use the tools, beliefs and practices I describe here to discover, connect and align your values, behaviours and purpose, so that your character enables you to actualise your mission on this planet.

STEP 1: RECOGNISE YOUR DEFAULT SETTINGS

The default setting of your SOS is usually indicated by your level of consciousness.

If you tend to avoid, ignore or refuse the concept that, as a human being, we are part of a bigger and wider system, then all you care about are your personal interests. Your level of consciousness will mainly focus on your ego, and you will make choices according to the immediate needs of your ego.

However, the higher your level of consciousness and the bigger and wider the system you can see, the more you will start to care about the wellbeing of others.

Now let's look at a couple of tools that will help you assess the default setting of your SOS.

Tool 1: The Barrett model

The Barrett model was created by Richard Barrett and is one of my favourite tools to support business leaders to transform their company's performance via development of their personal consciousness level, which works by shining a light on their desired core values.

When running a business, your core values play a vital role in the background.

Starting from day one, 'what you truly care about' provides the unwritten rules of your business. It influences the decisions, actions and behaviours of your people, and provides the guiding principles in terms of how your teams work together. It becomes the fundamental belief your team holds.

To make your company's culture work for you, start from knowing your personal core values. Where do these sit in terms of your level of consciousness? Are you motivated by ego-driven needs, which serve your personal interests, or by your spiritual-driven needs, which serve others' interests?

Free assessment is offered by Barrett Values Centre to help individuals understand their core values. You can find that here: https://www.valuescentre.com/tools-assessments/pva/.

However, if you are serious about finding the alignment between your core values, decisions, business culture, and overall business performance, it is worth investing in a proper 360-assessment so that your people are on the same page with you.

Tool 2: VIA character assessment

Character strengths are the traits that contribute to your good character.

The VIA Institute was set up by Martin Seligman, the father of positive psychology, and Neal Mayerson. According to research conducted by the Institute, every human being possesses twenty-four character strengths in various degrees. Being aware of these strengths, and how to apply them in life and at work, helps to identify purpose and meaning, and enhances wellbeing and positive emotions.

Free assessment can be accessed here:

https://www.viacharacter.org/account/register

STEP 2: PLUG IN NEW BELIEFS

As with upgrading other operating systems, to upgrade our SOS, we can start with the software of the system – beliefs. You need to dismiss the old, false beliefs that came with the default settings of your SOS, and plug in the new ones described in this section.

Belief 1: Everything is interconnected

Everything is indeed interconnected.

Albert Einstein once said:

> 'A human being is a part of the whole called by us universe, a part limited in time and space. He experiences himself, his thoughts and feelings as something separated from the rest, a kind of optical delusion of his consciousness. This delusion is a kind of prison for us, restricting us to our

personal desires and to affection for a few persons nearest to us. Our task must be to free ourselves from this prison by widening our circle of compassion to embrace all living creatures and the whole of nature in its beauty.'

Let me explain...

You may think your body is yours, completely yours, right?

But this is not true.

Your body is composed of cells and microbiomes, and the microbiomes outnumber the human cells! These cells and microbiomes are fed by and grow from the nutrients you consume. Those nutrients come from the vegetables, fruit, nuts and animals growing in the farms, and they are fed and grow from what is offered by nature... So, what makes up you doesn't come from you – it comes from the resources outside of you.

You may think your clothes are yours.

Yes, you purchased your clothes, but they were made from resources outside of you. The fabric and materials may be from plants or animals, and be produced in factories or be hand-made, but inevitably they pass through many hands before arriving in your wardrobe.

The same applies to the coffee you drink, the food you eat, the chair you sit on, the bed you sleep in, as well as the products or services your company sells and makes a profit from. All the things we consider to be ours are not; they came from and through many others ... others whom we don't know and know nothing about.

However, the choices made by those people we don't know also have an impact on us. For example, if farmers choose to use antibiotics to protect the pigs or cows or chickens on their farms from infection, those antibiotics get into our body when that pig or cow or chicken gets onto our plate. In recent years, there has been huge debate about the antibiotics used in food production. Some see it as a cause of serious illness in humans, while others believe the low dose used won't harm us. But while science is collecting data to catch up, it's no excuse for you to ignore the connection, right?

When we see the interconnection in all things we do and consume, it would be quite natural for us, as business leaders, to ask:

- What is my contribution to this interconnectedness?
- Does the choice I make here and now impose a positive or negative impact on the community or society there and then? What specifically might that impact be?
- When I am pursuing my success and happiness, am I costing others' wellbeing?
- How do my actions impact others' welfare specifically?

When you see the interconnections between everything and everyone, and see that we are all interrelated and interdependent, you may feel empowered to be here, on this planet, to do what you are meant to do and to make it better.

In 2017, I organised a conference – Neuroscience for Leaders – and the theme for that year was 'Unlocking your brain's true power to understand why and how everything is interconnected'. One of the speakers I engaged showed a short video of Earth, made by millions of pictures taken by a NASA engineer in space. It was not a fancy video; it simply showed Earth turning, bit by bit. The blue planet we are all living on slowly revolved, frame by frame. This short video, which didn't even come with any sound, made hundreds of people in the audience cry and smile at the same time.

Seeing the interconnections between everything and everyone, and realising that you are part of the people and the planet, will help you to ponder your purpose and the role you play in the system.

Belief 2: We are all soul mates

The term 'soul mate' has been traditionally used to describe your life partner, but I like to use it differently.

There are billions of people on the planet, and I would like to believe that if we have the chance to meet and interact – whether that's for a long or short time – that we are soul mates. We need each other to co-create the experiences that enable us to learn and grow. So we have a role to play in each interaction we have with another soul. We have responsibilities, even if, most of the time, we are not consciously aware of that.

For example, if you disagree with me, it's not because you're a bad person who wants to upset me. What is happening is that we have co-created a situation in which you are helping me to learn to see the situation from different angles, to improve my skills and to take multiple perspectives.

If you have done something wrong by me, it is not because you are an evil person with a malicious purpose. It is that we have co-created a situation for me to learn to manage my impulses, to articulate my needs, to set boundaries, to be assertive and to forgive.

If you betrayed me, it is not that you are a horrible, untrustworthy person. It is that we co-created a situation through which I can meet my strong emotions and get to know them intimately, regardless of whether it is grief, sadness, hate or anger. Such experience helps me to understand what is truly important to me, and practise self-compassion as well as forgiveness and hope.

We can only know ourselves deeply from these life experiences, and we need our soul mate(s) to co-create those experiences with us. We are mates at the soul level, and we are coming together on this planet to be part of each other's growth!

I wasn't born with this belief; I adopted it when I was experiencing a mid-life crisis at twenty-two. With no one around me to understand my frustration, I reached out to books to find insights. In one book I read about a young girl who lost her mother in her teens. The daughter was angry with her mum, as she felt she was abandoned. She attended a workshop hosted by a well-known medium, who claimed that he could communicate with the spirits of people who had passed away. The girl asked the medium to ask her mother, 'How could you have abandoned me?!' The answer she got from her mum's spirit stayed with me for twenty years, and went something like this:

'We all come to Earth to have experiences, because our souls need those lessons to learn and grow. Your lessons are different from mine; that's why we have different experiences. I didn't abandon you, but maybe loss and grief are the lessons your soul needs to learn through this experience...'

Boom!

When you believe that we are all soul mates to each other, the way we live together on this planet changes. You understand that we are more like souls who come here to study together. We are mates who laugh and cry together, who fight and support each other. We play different roles that might lift someone up or bring someone down. The point is not whether others are good or bad mates. The point is what we learn from the experiences we co-create.

The experiences we have are like the selective subjects we enrolled in at university. Our soul selected the subjects for us, and we must get a pass before moving on to the next one. Whoever co-created a situation – an experience that will help us to learn and graduate from that class – are the people we need to thank, for they are the mates for our souls.

Belief 3: You are here to make a positive difference

I don't know about you, but in my younger days the pure thought that I was born by accident and would have to live on this planet for about seventy or eighty years, experience endless ups and downs, feel both happiness and sadness, and go through countless difficulties and challenges made Earth sound like hell to me. I must have been a weird and reserved kid, because I kept asking 'Why?!' Why do we have to go through all the pain and difficulty? What's the purpose of coming here and living here for that many years?'

After spending countless time questioning and pondering, the answer that finally satisfied me is that 'we are here to make a difference'!

You, me, none of us, would need to be here if our lives didn't serve a certain purpose. Whatever the purpose is, in serving that purpose we make a difference in our own life, the lives of those around us, and the whole of humanity and the world at large.

However, don't confuse 'making a difference' with 'changing the world' immediately on a global scale. You don't need to overwhelm yourself by looking at it that way; instead, think about how you can make a difference in what you can control now. For example:

- Choose to become a better, sweeter person after experiencing hardship, instead of becoming a sad, bitter person.

- Choose to pick up the trash, to pay it forward, to reach out and lend a hand, to be there when you are needed, and to give and share without expecting anything in return.
- Choose to be mindful of the energy brought into the space you step into. Ask yourself, 'Would being judgemental, cynical and negative be the energy that can make a positive impact on others?'
- Choose to be mindful of the choices you make that may have wider impact on the people and community outside your inner circle.

Basically, act out your core values and stand fast to your principles. As a business leader, when you are crystal clear about this, you will be able to run a mission-first business – a business that is not just about making profit, but also involved in making positive differences in society.

Making a positive difference in the world on a big scale starts by making a positive change in yourself first, and then in your circle, in your work and in your community.

The moment you believe the purpose of your presence is to make a positive difference, you will change your approach to life and work. Think about it. If you believe that you are here to make a positive difference, would you:

- Be mean to the people around you?
- Tell big or small lies to get what you want?
- Play within the grey areas to get ahead?
- Ignore others' interests and take shortcuts for personal convenience?
- Compete to win at the expenses of others?

- Make a profit by taxing people and/or the planet?

We are all here to make a difference, good or bad, so make your choice wisely.

STEP 3: EMPLOY NEW PRACTICES

Now that you have identified the default settings of your SOS and been introduced to new beliefs, it's time to get practical. The rest of this chapter outlines practices you can employ to assist the continual upgrading of your SOS.

Practice 1: Cherish silence and solitude

Many great spiritual traditions honour the practice of silence and solitude as a way to deepen the connection to our innermost selves.

Within each of us, there is a silence, a silence as vast as the universe. And when we experience that silence, we remember who we are...

— GUNILLA NORRIS

Silence is the journey to find self.

In silence, you can hear your thoughts more clearly. As discussed earlier, your thoughts are associated with your feelings, your feelings drive you to take actions, and your actions deliver results. Only when in solitude do you have the chance to dive down and discover the beliefs and values that shape your thoughts, to understand where they come from, and to reveal what they do to you today.

Silence and solitude are the doorway that we walk through to connect our inner world with our outer experiences. They are necessary for our wellbeing and potential success. Bill Gates regularly spends two weeks in the woods to read, to reflect, to think. It is important to get away from noise so that deep thinking becomes possible and effective.

But you don't need two weeks in the woods; all you need to do is NOT fill the gaps.

If you pay attention, you may notice that we have a tendency to 'fill the gaps' when it's quiet. We turn the TV or radio on, arrange parties, make phone calls and have conversations for the sake of having conversations. We do everything to fill the gap, to keep our five senses busy.

I remember that after I finished my first vipassana – a ten-day silent meditation course – the first change I made in my routine was to turn off the radio in the car on my hour-long drive home from the retreat centre. I used to find that drive boring, so I played music, listened to podcasts and made phone calls to fill the gap. But now I prefer driving in silence, so that I can meet my soul.

If you are quite busy, schedule and block time on your calendar to have an inward journey, and make it your non-negotiable top priority.

Here are a couple of tips on how to take that inward journey:

- Spend time in nature in silence.

  You can run, hike or ride your bike in a nearby park or on a nature trail, or simply take a stroll in your garden. The point is to mute your phone and block out all distractions during that time so that you can immerse yourself in nature.

Immersion in nature offers a sense of connection and oneness with all beings. Solitude is also a door to self-connection. So make sure you check in on yourself.

- Spend a few minutes taking a break in your office.

  Close the door behind you, close your eyes, and take a sensory break. Breathe deeply and slowly, listening to the silence and noticing the thoughts that pop into your mind. Pay attention to the sensations in your body and experience the feelings that come to you ... then, express your gratitude or love.

- Guard empty space on your calendar.

  Busy and driven leaders tend to fill up all the spaces on their calendar, because, of course, we should always be engaged in doing something to achieve something.

  More than once, when I have asked a client to show me their calendar, it made my heart race because their schedule is so crazy! They don't just double book – they triple book themselves! Any human being with a logical mind would agree that you can't be in two meetings at the same time, let alone three.

  'Can you create some blank space on your calendar? Fifteen to thirty minutes a day would do,' I often ask my clients.

  They often resist and say, 'But I am already quite busy. How would a blank space help?'

  But I insist. 'Give it a try next week, and see what happens,' I say.

  And the next week they often say to me, 'It turned out

that I don't need to be in so many meetings! And I have been able to use that "blank spot" to re-orient/settle/ground myself.'

Practice 2: Own your experiences

I hope that now you have read this far, you can agree that we create our own reality. That you understand that to own your experience is to take responsibility for your experience. Because whatever you have experienced in the outside world stems from the unique value system that sits inside you.

Owning your experiences means taking personal responsibility to align your values and behaviours. This will allow you to achieve what you consciously want to achieve, be aware of the effect of your choices and actions on others, and better yourself without taxing other people or the planet or the society that current and future generations live in.

To own your experience requires you to know your **WHY**, **WHAT** and **HOW**.

Knowing self is a journey; it requires constant enquiry. If you only dabble, you won't get past this practice either, because truly knowing self requires discipline, courage and persistence.

Knowing your big WHY may inspire you to take more challenges, to stretch yourself, to make yourself more resilient, and to gather your energy and strength to invest in delivering the things that are much bigger than you.

So, what are your goals, dreams and desires? A simple question, right? Well, what I have observed is that not everyone has a clear idea of what they want.

I trust you have met people who don't know their WHY and WHAT – people who are not conscious of why they do what they do and what they really want for themselves. In the workplace and in society, they function as sleepwalkers.

I trust you also have met the cousin of the sleepwalker, who is working on others' WHATS.

When we are working on others' WHATS, it's like we're walking on a path that has already been laid out, and all you need to do is follow it. And if you walk this path you may do it well, but because the path is not yours, even if you achieve great results you won't have that sense of fulfilment.

Did you spend years getting a degree or running a business that you had no passion for at all? But you did it because your family told you to or your friends or someone you know seemed to have a great life doing it.

As a business owner, you can also make the mistake of following others' WHATS.

Have you ever jumped into setting up a business because someone else made a fortune in that line of work? Have you ever headhunted a star performer from another business and hoped and wished he or she would be a star in your team as well? Have you ever copied and pasted a strategy that brings huge success in others' businesses with the expectation that it would do so in yours?

Remember Mark, whom we met at the start of the chapter? His strategy was to 'extend the business into the relevant industry and recruit a group of bright and hard-working professionals'. It was a brilliant idea, but poorly executed. Any business that expands into a new market or industry and adds hundreds of new employees in just a few months usually experiences diluted core values and culture, which are the soul of the business. When the soul is missing, dreams and ambitions lack a solid ground to stand on. In a business context, when the WHY and HOW are twisted, despite the professionalism of WHO and WHAT, the effort we make won't deliver the results we want.

The same concept applies to Mark's 'marketing activities'. By investing in superficial marketing activities that presented him as a relatable leader who showed he cares about his people by meeting with them at their desks or showering them with gifts on their birthdays, Mark missed the opportunity to truly bond deeply with his employees. He was unable to discover why those people were willing to work with him and support the business in the first place. When Mark missed the opportunity to create alignment between his own deeds and values and extend that into his business, the persona he invested in creating went out the window.

Working on your own WHAT is more like allowing the path to unfold in front of you. You may not be able to define it immediately, but keep searching and questioning along the way and you may just find it.

Here is a practice to help you own your experiences and find your WHAT. Write down the following questions on a notepad and put them in the back of your mind. Carry them with you as if you are lightly holding something precious in your hand, and be open to receive the answers.

- Do I know what I don't want? (If you do, flip it.)
- Am I working on a WHAT that sounds like a SHOULD?
- Am I mistaking 'being inspired' for 'mimicking'?
- What do I want despite my fears?

If you manage to get clear on your WHY and WHAT, you can work out your HOW. As psychiatrist and Holocaust survivor Dr

Viktor Frankl once wrote, 'He who has a why can bear any how.'

When you devise your HOW, make character your loudest statement at all times.

Character comprises the qualities and nature that are distinctive to who you are, and it motivates what you do when you have nothing to gain. Your character is specific, personal and yours. It is linked closely to reputation. It is how you are known. It's the mental image that first comes to mind when people think about you. And it determines what you get from life.

When you lead your team and business, take time to make mindful choices in the middle of chaos by asking yourself:

- What motivates me to ...?
- What are my character strengths?
- How can I use my character strengths creatively in this situation?

So, if you know Mark, you will know that he gathered his courage to face the problem and invited forty employees to participate in 360-degree reviews of his behaviours. Although he was gutted by the result, he presented it to his leadership team and said, 'I am the problem. I need your help to correct that.'

Practice 3: Recognise the voice of your ego

Deepak Chopra once said in an interview, 'If you want to reach a state of bliss, go beyond your ego.'

As you already know, your ego's job is to protect you. But it needs to be managed. Otherwise, it will over-protect us and therefore limit us.

Did you grow up with over-protective parents? Parents who

loved you so much that they perceived everything you experienced as potentially dangerous, and so they stopped you from living your life? Such parents control what you eat, wear and do because they believe that only what they give you is the best. They question what you want to eat, wear and do because such things are *not* the best.

When we have over-protective parents, as we grow up, we rebel. We fight to protect our right to decide what to eat, wear and do. And just as you did as a teenager, you may also be doing so in your adulthood. We set up boundaries, we negotiate and renegotiate, so that our loving parents can love us in the way that enables us, not limits us.

Well, this is what you need to do with your ego.

It is challenging and at times painful to acknowledge and address the different ways our ego keeps us feeling 'separate' – when it declares we are 'unique' and 'the best' and don't have to take responsibility for the hurt we cause others or, conversely, that we are 'defective' and 'not good enough' and have to take responsibility for everyone's hurt. But there is a liberation in truly knowing ourselves and challenging the ego's portrait of who we are.

So, listen to yourself and check in on your ego regularly. Here are a few questions to gauge whether your ego is talking:

- Are you pursuing a goal to feel superior and have more glory?
- In the face of uncertainty, are you speaking to yourself in a fearful and anxious way?
- Do you hear yourself speak in judgement or comparison?
- Do you lie, spin or brag a bit to feel good about yourself?
- Do you speak to yourself in a way that makes you feel insecure, inadequate, or not enough?

- After making a decision, do you notice that you back it up with a long list of justifications?
- Do you hate being told that you have made a mistake, even if all the facts prove that?
- Do you need constant recognition and validation to be motivated to do what you are doing?
- Do you feel it is very painful to ask for help or receive feedback?
- Do people around you keep saying, 'Don't take it personally'?

When you hear the voice of your ego, simply acknowledge it, then let it go. You can acknowledge it and let it go by saying to it: 'I see you, I know you want to protect me, but I'm safe and well, so let me handle this.'

Practice 4: Assume positive intent

Remember Indra Nooyi, the former CEO of PepsiCo that I mentioned previously? When she was asked by *Fortune* magazine what the most important leadership advice she had been given was, she said, 'Whatever anybody says or does, assume positive intent.'

As humans, we tend to project unwanted characteristics onto others. As explained in psychology, we unconsciously do so to protect ourselves from having to acknowledge parts of the self that we don't like. As human beings, we also tend to notice and focus more on negativity. Often that negativity can manifest in snap judgements, playing the blame game and making erroneous assumptions about others, especially in tense situations.

If someone's behaviour is different from ours, instead of asking questions to understand their intentions, it's easy to conclude that they are bad people with an evil soul. Let's use Stella, a hard-working manager, as an example:

Stella cares about relationships, so she prioritises her time and invests energy in building good relationships with others at work. However, in the past few years the leadership survey conducted with her team, colleagues and managers all pointed to one thing: Stella is quite negative. Which is quite shocking for Stella!

Through conversations with Stella, it became clear that the way she chose to build good relationships was undermining her!

When building relationships with people, particularly when she had one-on-one conversations, she tended to badmouth third or fourth parties behind their back. She would make rude comments on their actions and assume they had evil intentions. For example, she thinks people are criticising her when they asked questions about the project she is working on; she thinks others devalue her when they rescheduled a meeting with her ... Stella thought that analysing or judging someone negatively and sharing her frustration about who was not present would bring her closer to the people she was in conversation with, but, unfortunately, it does the opposite!

Assuming others have positive intent, even if they behave differently from us, is instrumental in cultivating trust. It is rooted in a belief that we are all the same – that is, we all want to do well and be better, just like you do.

During my time on this planet, I haven't yet met one person who wakes up in the morning and decides: 'I'm going to be a bad person today. I'll make choices that hurt others and make them miserable. YES! That's the goal for today!' Have you met someone like this? I doubt it.

The reason we behave differently and make different choices all comes down to the perspectives we take, and the level of competencies we have mastered to carry out our intentions. But perspectives are meant to be different, and competency levels vary as well. People are hardly born with the skills to behave in the way that pleases everybody.

When we choose to explain others' behaviour in a negative way, we unconsciously put roadblocks in the way of our ability to trust others, as well as make ourselves less trustworthy.

In the book *The Speed of Trust*, Stephen Covey says that *'we judge ourselves according to our intentions, but we judge other people according to their behaviour and make assumptions about their intentions.'* So others can be stupid, careless, selfish, insincere, political … we assume and make conclusions about others' personalities, character and values. But all we get from doing this is plenty of imagined enemies instead of allies.

So, instead of automatically assuming negative intent, assume positive intent. Which means:

- Trying to capture yourself in the moment of assuming negative intent.
- Pausing and asking yourself, 'Is this a fact or an assumption?' rather than immediately taking action sparked by the strong emotions that come with your assumptions.
- Checking your assumptions by talking to the person directly, not behind their back.
- Being curious, and listening to people to understand why they do what they choose to do and what they want to achieve.

If, after careful assessment, evil intent is confirmed, then accept it and move on. But allow yourself the chance to double check and continue to practise 'assuming positive intent'. This practice is the seed that will grow into trust and true collaboration.

Practice 5: Embrace oneness

We are here to awaken from the illusion of separateness.

— THICH NHAT HANH

Embracing oneness is the action you take to reflect that we are ONE.

As human beings, we have similar life experiences: we go through ups and downs, we experience joy and anger, we seek to be respected and cared for. We contribute to each other's life experiences and are also influenced and affected by the actions and decisions made by others. We are interconnected and interdependent, while at the same time we are self-dependent to create and co-create our experiences on this planet.

From a spiritual point of view, oneness is to have a deep understanding of the fact that, regardless of how different we are from each other, in many ways we are the same – we all seek love, respect and happiness, we all face similar challenges, we all deal with similar pains and go through similar stages in life to evolve.

Embracing oneness has several aspects.

On one hand, long-lasting success mean more than just making loads of money. It includes having all aspects of your life working together: business, family, relationships and your place in the community. The reality is that for us to be truly fulfilled – not just have moments or periods of fleeting success or happiness – we must do more than just build our success at the expense of others. We cannot just serve ourselves – we also need to serve others.

Serving others and serving ourselves are the two sides of the same coin, in my view.

When we believe in 'oneness', then there's no division. When we're serving to support others, we take the focus off ourselves, and serving other people is a different vehicle to make ourselves better.

It might sound counter-intuitive, but focusing on serving others can actually be more profitable than focusing on profit only when you are running a business. If you focus on bettering others' lives, you will be rewarded with the insights and wisdom to figure out how to grow a more monetarily lucrative business. Because the best way to make money is to solve problems for others, the bigger and wider the problem is, the more significant the potential profit. The more value you can add for others, the more you will be compensated.

On the other hand, it is also true that to produce the most 'selfless' results, you have to serve yourself first and serve yourself in the proper way. That is, to best serve others, you have to care for yourself and do the kind of work that's truly right for you.

Serving yourself the right way means taking ample time to focus on your self-development, rather than immediately seeking out ways to help others. I often encounter passionate professionals who say, 'Aw, I just want to help others, I want to be the light for others!' The thing is, the original purpose of the light is not to light the path for others. It is to help you find the path in darkness, to find the order in chaos. When you do that for yourself, helping others will come as a natural by-product. Your experiences are valuable for others, so after you have walked through the darkness you can light up the path for others. It is never the other way around.

Serving yourself also means taking time to develop your core values, discover your strengths and passion, and cultivate skills and habits around those insights. It means taking care of yourself, which includes physical practices like hygiene, diet and exercise, as well as mental facets like meditation, relaxation and anything else that's beneficial to your soul.

Embracing oneness means we are ONE. Each of us is a tiny aspect of the whole, so what I do to you, I do to myself, and vice versa.

What's next?

When you start to upgrade your SOS, you are able to connect the dots. You admit that there are things – **connections** – that you don't know about but want to know about. You become curious. You seek meaningful connections with something bigger than yourself and find your position in this bigger system, which takes commitment and effort.

Upgrading your spiritual operating system provides you with the eyes of your BEING. This leads to positive relationships, higher self-esteem, greater optimism and the ability to follow a strong purpose in life. It gives you a sense of peace, wholeness and balance among the physical, emotional, social and spiritual aspects of your life.

Seeing the interconnectedness of all life can also help buffer the pain that comes with difficult experiences. As researcher Kristin Neff says:

> 'If we can compassionately remind ourselves in moments of falling down that failure is part of the shared human experience, then that moment becomes one of togetherness rather than isolation. When our troubled, painful experiences are framed by the recognition that countless others have undergone similar hardships, the blow is softened.' [8]

Connecting the dots between your core values, your character, your decisions and your life experiences helps you see the big picture and know the role you are playing in it. It allows you to gain clarity and see the consequences of the choices you make in the moment. You are making a contribution as well as receiving the compensation.

Here is a simple self-assessment to understand the current state of your SOS.

Self-assessment: Spiritual Operating System

The scale for each statement is 1–5.
1 = the statement does NOT resonate with me at all
5 = the statement describes exactly the way things are in my life

	1	2	3	4	5
1. I have a strong sense of purpose, and people who know me say I am very mission oriented.					
2. I'm making life decisions according to my values.					
3. I'm fearless when my heart says 'Yes'.					
4. I feel fulfilled and my heart is at peace all the time.					
5. I'm contributing to society and serving my community with generosity.					
6. I attract and support those whose causes are inspiring.					
7. I'm attractive to others due to my virtues and character.					

My score is: _____

Chapter 3

Emotional Operating System

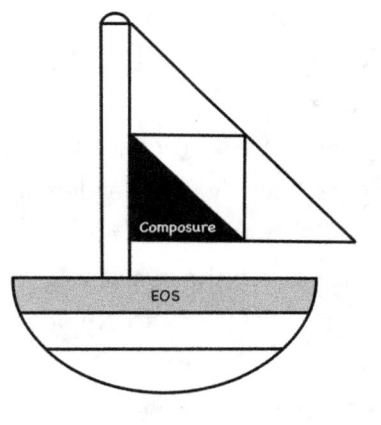

Everything that irritates us about others can lead to
an understanding of ourselves.

— CARL JUNG

When I first met Leo, he was an overweight, short-tem-
pered executive who had single-handedly established a
business in a highly competitive industry. He had over 150
young, bright and ambitious professionals working under
him, and they were successfully serving the most demanding luxury brands on the planet.

But he had problems – particularly with his temper.

'When an employee comes to my door and asks stupid questions, I just want to throw myself out of the window,' he said. And his office was on level twenty-six of a tall building downtown.

Leo was becoming unhappy with his team's performance, and he easily lost his temper in the office. He didn't like coming to the office, but he had to, and when he saw people lined up outside his door to ask him questions, he immediately felt agitated. 'I need help', he said, 'but don't ask me to exercise.'

So I did a 360-interview to understand the business, the operation, and particularly Leo's leadership style. During the interviews, I discovered that Leo was a hard-working perfectionist. He started the business with two partners, then quickly expanded into a 150-employee team within three years.

Due to his hard work and perfectionism, the company's designing was highly appreciated by demanding luxury brands that care about meticulous details. But the more contracts Leo signed and the more demanding the job became, the more easily Leo lost his temper in front of his team. Several of Leo's direct reports said that the fights between Leo and other executives were low and personal. But it hadn't always been that way...

'I want our culture back,' Leo said to me. 'We were the company that offered the best design in town, but now our people don't care about the quality!'

Leo was struggling to continue with the business, even to show up in the office when he was most needed. He felt powerless, frustrated, helpless, and he wanted to withdraw.

Meet your messenger

Emotions are what make life worth living, and sometimes worth ending.

The Emotional Operating System (**EOS**) is invisible, but it helps us to take actions, to survive, to strike to avoid danger, to make decisions, and to understand and motivate ourselves, as well as others. The EOS is in charge of your feelings, attitudes and actions, it affects and influences your physical body, and can be influenced by your mental and spiritual operating systems as well.

The American Psychological Association (APA) defines emotion as 'a complex reaction pattern involving experiential, physiological, and behavioural elements.'[9]

The '**experiential**' component refers to the stimuli that can trigger subjective emotional experiences inside you. This could be finding a beautiful waterfall at the end of a hiking trail, seeing your company's share price go up or slide down, tasting the wedding cake at your best friend's wedding, or hearing your colleague misinterpreting your intention.

The '**physiological**' component refers to the involuntary bodily reactions we have when we are having the subjective emotional experiences. They are involuntary and you cannot choose or control them – the autonomic nervous system controls them. An example is the fight or flight reaction your body has when you sense immediate danger – such as being confronted by a hungry lion. Your heartbeat might go up, the rhythm of your breathing may change, your palms may start to sweat, and you may feel tightness in your muscles. This reaction primes you to run away from the lion. In modern urban life you won't see hungry lions wandering the streets, but your fight or flight reaction can still be triggered by perceived dangers. These include such things as a car speeding towards you, or a request to make a speech in front of a bunch of important investors. Perceived dangers to your psychological safety are as real as those to your physical safety.

The physiological component of emotion also includes more subtle sensations. When the neurotransmitters, chemicals and hormones related to emotion are moving around inside you, you may notice heat, tension, or a tickling sensation like tiny ants moving around on your skin. Those sensations are subtle, and the majority of people today only notice them through deliberate practice.

The '**behavioural**' component of emotion refers to the action we take in response to the emotion. In the case of being confronted by a hungry lion or speeding car, the response may well be to run away from the lion, or jump away from the car. The behaviour can also be a facial expression, such as a frown or smile; a body movement, such as throwing your arms around somebody; or a sound you make, such as shouting or screaming. It can also be the decisions you make, such as refusing to give the requested speech.

In Leo's case, he was constantly experiencing anger at work and the behavioural component of his anger included yelling at employees, dismissing their proposals, and shutting up a colleague or even the entire team.

So, from the subjective experience to the physiological reactions, to the behaviours that we consciously or automatically choose to put forward, emotions work closely with our five senses. As the energy moves around our body, it carries information received from the five senses that notifies us of what is happening in the environment. This facilitates quick communication between our brain and body, so that we can choose an action and respond to what is happening.

In that sense, emotion is a messenger. Do you agree?

HOW YOUR EOS WORKS

To fully understand the emotional operating system, we need first to understand the hardware it uses: the brain.

There are parts of the brain that play a significant role in our emotional process.

It's useful to understand the concept of the triune brain, which was proposed by the neuroscientist Paul MacLean in the 1960s. He suggested that when we consider the overall functionality of the brain, we can look at three layers, each of which was developed according to evolutionary needs and carries specific functionality to meet those needs. These days, there are researchers who argue that the triune brain is no longer the most accurate model of the brain, but it is still a compelling model that helps us understand the basics of brain evolution.[10] Let's have a look.

From the bottom up, the three layers of brain are:

The **reptilian brain** is the oldest part of the brain and includes the basal ganglia and brain stem. It's in charge of our involuntary and instinctual behaviours, such as heart rate, breathing and balance.

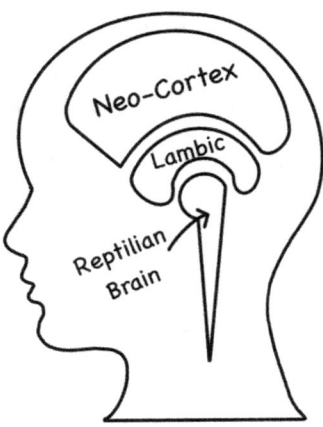

The **limbic system**, which sits in the middle of the brain, includes the amygdala, hippocampus, hypothalamus and cingulate gyrus. It plays a significant role in human emotions.

The **neocortex**, the uppermost layer of the brain, is the youngest, and is where complex thinking, language, social abilities and self-control and regulation come from.

These lower layers of the brain – that is, the reptilian brain and limbic system – operate below your consciousness. On the one hand, this is good, as we don't have to actually remember to breathe or make our heart beat. But on the other hand, this can create trouble for us, because when reactions are unconscious it is harder for us to detect and manage them.

The part of the brain that we are most concerned with here is the limbic system – the middle layer – which is where your emotions are processed and which influences your choice of actions. For that reason, the limbic system is known for many as the 'emotional centre' of the brain.

Several structures in the limbic system developed to enable us to respond to important needs, such as searching for food and dealing with life-threatening dangers, as well as ensuring that we reproduce. The key structures in the limbic system are the amygdala and hypothalamus, which function as an alarm system for perceived dangers and threats. But there are some defects in this system.

Just like the smoke detector in your kitchen, the amygdala functions 24/7 to scan its surroundings. If the amygdala detects anything **SIMILAR** to dangerous situations experienced in the past, it signals the hypothalamus to initiate the survival protocol automatically. '**Similar**' is the key word here, and it is also where the 'defects' come from.

For evolutionary purposes, the limbic system functions on the principle of 'rather be safe than sorry', so it tends to be activated by benign factors as well as real threats. This is why sometimes we find ourselves jumping and screaming at the sight of a long, green, winding tube in the garden, only to realise it is a water hose, not a snake.

The limbic system is interconnected with the neocortex, which is the part of the brain that makes us human and is also the most recently developed part of the brain. The prefrontal cortex (PFC) is the part of the neocortex that sits in the very front of the brain, just behind your forehead, and is where thinking, planning, learning, analysing, solving problems and making decisions takes place. This is why, when the prefrontal cortex steps in, we feel embarrassed for jumping and screaming at a snake-like garden hose.

The battle of the brains

Biologically, your ability to manage your emotional impulses is about the battle between your prefrontal cortex and limbic system. The prefrontal cortex earned the nickname 'the CEO of the brain'

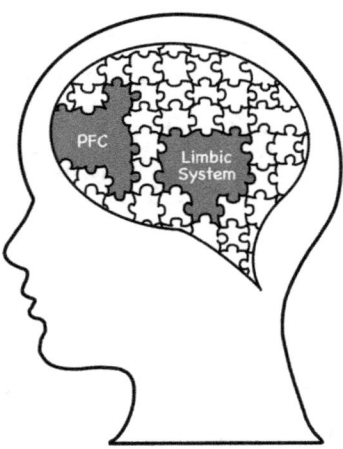

because the functions it carries out are mainly related to short-term memory, problem solving, analysing, reasoning, impulse control, planning and implementing.

In an ideal world, our conscious mind is always in control and our prefrontal cortex will always regulate the activation of the amygdala in the limbic system. But in reality, this isn't always the case. In a stressful situation, blood supply to the frontal lobes and prefrontal cortex is reduced, meaning it's harder to think and plan and decide which behaviours to display. When this happens, the amygdala overrides the prefrontal cortex to hijack control of the stress response. This is what is happening when you are caught up by your emotions and say or do things WITHOUT thinking that you may regret afterwards. This is called 'amygdala hijack' – your prefrontal cortex is hijacked by the amygdala.

This 'amygdala hijack' can happen for several reasons. For example, when:

- Your brain is tired because you've spent lots of time thinking and working. Road rage on the way home after a long day at work is an example of a tired PFC not having the strength to control an outburst.

- Your PFC is impaired due to your lifestyle. When the cortex gets thinner, it's harder for the PFC to control the amygdala. Research has proved that regular intake of alcohol kills neurons in the brain and leads to increased stress reactions in the body. It is not surprising that people who have drinking issues also have anger management issues.
- Your amygdala is too active. Later we will discuss venting, which can make your amygdala over-sensitive to triggers. The more sensitive it gets, the more energy the PFC has to consume to manage it.

Do you remember Leo from the story at the beginning of this chapter? His impression about certain executives was that they didn't take ownership of their work and didn't care about details and quality. The moment his brain sensed the cues that indicated these attitudes, he lashed out at them and turned the meeting room, metaphorically, into a blood-filled battlefield. His prefrontal cortex was hijacked by his amygdala.

It's important to understand that emotions are a brief episode of coordinated and autonomic brain activities and behavioural changes that facilitate a response to an event. They are lower-level responses, coded in our genes. Regardless of how rational we believe we are, we all have to accept that we are capable of irrational behaviour.

It is not rare to see business leaders make fast decisions in the heat of the moment when their emotions are aroused, and leave important factors out. It is also not rare to see leaders jump to conclusions and push themselves to make significant decisions when they are stressed and tired and, inevitably, make mistakes.

In the business world and in life, most of us also keep making a crucial mistake. When we try to influence or persuade others, we tend to focus on rational factors and ignore feelings and emotions. But feelings and emotions are the actual drivers of decision making. Harvard professor Gerald Zaltman, the author of a ground-breaking book, *How Customers Think: Essential Insights into the Mind of the Markets*, revealed that almost ninety per cent of the decisions we make are based on emotion, not rationality.

When building your business and leading a team, you are bound to fail if you keep ignoring the role emotions play.

DEFAULT SETTINGS OF THE EOS

In my line of work, I have had the privilege to support mid-senior business leaders and founders. It is not an easy job that they do, if you ask me.

Running a business feels like you are living in two separate worlds. In one, there are endless tasks and problems waiting for your intervention. In the other, there are the emotional challenges of being the leader. You carry a deep burden to deliver and achieve while also being filled with joy for the opportunity. You are expected to address problems in a sober-minded way while also rejoicing when good things happen.

Leading a business is not easy, but it's even harder if your emotional operating system is falling back on its default modes. You may let your strong emotions choose which behaviours to display. Like Leo, you may find yourself shouting and slamming doors. Such colourful behaviour is usually followed by employees gossiping about you at the water cooler – as they did with Leo – with the result being long-lasting damage to your personal brand. And we don't want that to happen to you. So...

Let's now look at the common default settings of business leaders I have encountered.

Ignoring or suppressing emotions

In theory, you may know it's not healthy to ignore an emotion because, again, in theory, you may know that it's likely to surface later without the benefit of processing and learning from it. But the reality is that leaders tend to ignore emotions, because trying to process them is inconvenient when you have a long list of tasks to execute. So, you try not to pay attention to them, and hope they go away so that you can focus on finishing what is urgent and important.

Really?

It is true that all emotions are temporary. However, ignoring them will cost you – big time!

Research has discovered that pushing your emotions down where no one, including yourself, will ever find them, will contribute negatively to your mental health. Emotions are the physiological sensations created by the hormones moving inside your body. You can ignore them, but they will travel inside you anyway.

Imagine your physical body is a stable and your emotions are the captive horses inside. When emotions are strong, it's like the horses are trying to charge out of the stable. Suppressing and ignoring your emotions is like trying to force the door of the stable closed while the horses are kicking and neighing inside. You can imagine the damage they make as they try to get out.

There is nothing to be gained from suppressing emotions.

When you ignore and suppress your emotions, you numb your physical body so that you cannot connect your physical sensations with specific emotions and feelings. The longer you use this approach to deal with emotions, the more likely you are to feel like your temper comes storming out of nowhere with no warning, and you just cannot control it!

Of course, I'm not suggesting that you give your full attention to every single emotional experience, big or small, but if you're running a business and have a team working for you, it is critical to have clear criteria about which emotions can be ignored and which need attention.

Dismissing or minimising emotions

The academic name for dismissing and minimising emotions is emotional invalidation. It is the act of dismissing or rejecting someone else's, or our own, thoughts, feelings or behaviours.

You may find yourself saying to yourself or someone else, 'Oh, just let it go.' But what you are actually saying is, 'Your feelings don't matter. Your feelings are wrong.' And emotional invalidation isn't necessarily just verbal. Have you ever rolled your eyes at someone, or ignored them, or played on your phone while they're talking? Regardless of what form emotional validation takes – verbal or otherwise – it creates confusion and distrust.

You know that phrase 'what goes around comes around'? If you tend to invalidate emotions for others, you're very likely to do it to yourself as well. When you repeatedly invalidate the emotions you experience, you create confusion, self-doubt and distrust in your own emotions. It's like you're scolding yourself for even having feelings.

If you're the recipient of emotional invalidation, you may often hide your emotions and slowly and surely develop low self-esteem. If you tend to compare yourself with others; if you have problems asking for what you need; if you have trouble accepting compliments or positive feedback; if you have difficulty in establishing healthy boundaries; if you tend to avoid challenges or give up quickly without really trying ... you may find the reasons for and solutions to these issues if you look into how you deal with emotions.

Being ruled by emotions

Vicki Botnick, a therapist in Tarzana, California, explains that any emotion – even elation, joy, or others you'd typically view as positive – can intensify to a point where it becomes difficult to control.

How do you know you are ruled by emotions? The answer is simple – you're reacting instead of responding!

When you're ruled by your emotions, you react in the heat of the moment and say the first thing that pops into your head. As Leo said of his seemingly uncontrollable temper, 'I don't have control over it, I can feel my body shaking afterwards, and I can tell some of the words I chose were not the best, but I had no control of it at that moment.'

In that heated moment, jumping to conclusions feels so much easier than demonstrating grace and giving someone the benefit of the doubt. And you can't separate fact from fiction.

Feelings are the mental name we assign to the emotions we experience. They are not right or wrong – they're just feelings, and they cannot always be trusted. In fact, more often than not, our feelings could be lying to us.

When we're into it too deep, feelings begin to trump reality for us. Just because your employee looked at you in a funny way, or spoke with a sharp tone, doesn't mean that he or she doesn't respect you, but your strong feelings convince you otherwise.

Simply reacting may feel like an intuitive response in the moment, but it's important to understand that our feelings don't have to rule our behaviour. This is the first step towards updating your emotional operating system into a healthier version.

Projecting emotions onto others

Have you ever heard yourself saying, 'So and so made me upset.' Well, this sentence is not exactly correct. It implies the other person actually deliberately created a negative situation that made you feel an undue level of distress.

When we say these things it is an act of emotional projection. Emotional projection is the act of transferring the ownership of our emotions to others. So when we say, 'You made me sad,' or 'She made me angry,' we are actually saying, '*You* are responsible for how I feel, and since you made me feel bad, you are the person who shall be questioned or distanced.'

Alternatively, we may also believe we are responsible for how other people feel. As leaders, how many of us have hesitated to tell the truth because the truth hurts?

The reality is that you are the only person who can make you feel a certain way. All that others can do is create a situation.

The opposite of emotional projection is emotional responsibility, which means being accountable for not only your actions and behaviours, but also your thoughts and feelings. It is your responsibility to step back and step up, and believe that 'I take responsibility for how I feel.' For example, rather than saying, 'You made me miserable,' you say, 'I feel misery as a result of this situation.'

If you look more deeply, you will see that emotional responsibility is really just a belief in emotional independence: my emotions are wholly independent of your actions. And emotional projection is really just a belief in emotional dependence: my emotions are wholly dependent on your actions.

Believing strong emotions are bad

When we don't have enough skills to regulate emotions, positive or negative, we tend to believe all strong emotions, particularly those 'negative' ones, are the source of unhappiness and should be eliminated from our lives. So, when we have a negative emotion, we tend to hide it or avoid it. In fact, we may avoid situations or blame the people that trigger these strong 'negative' emotions.

When we try to hide or avoid strong emotions, we tend to create a space between ourselves and others. We build walls around ourselves, and consequently we feel distant from others. The thicker the wall becomes, the bigger the distance between ourselves and others becomes, and the harder it is for us to connect and bond with others. Emotional regulation seems to be a common problem among leaders. I have often been called in to help solve problematic behaviour in a workplace. I hate to say it, but it seems the more senior a person gets, the more their ability to utilise their emotions wisely diminishes.

Venting emotions

We've all had that experience of running to a good friend to vent and get things off our chest when something or someone makes us angry and frustrated. And, when the caring friend listens to us and immediately validates our feelings, we feel good and believe we are right to be upset.

However, there is scientific evidence that venting about your bad day or your irresponsible employee won't make you feel better in the long run, and in fact it could harm your brain.

Research published in the *Journal of Consulting and Clinical Psychology* suggests that talking about thoughts and feelings after a trauma, or 'venting', may not help (Seery et al., 2008). Worse, it may be psychologically damaging. A survey conducted after September 11 looked at how effective different coping strategies were. The study found that actively venting was a significant predictor of post-traumatic stress disorder (PTSD).[11]

When we vent, we might feel good in the moment, because we know we have someone there who we can rely on, who cares about us, who is willing to spare their precious time to listen to us. And that make us feel good, right? And if we vent to the right person in the right way, articulating and verbalising what happened can help us to see a situation more clearly, provide more perspectives and insights, and help us to process our emotions. However, this latter part of the equation often gets lost in the process of venting. Too often, we vent the 'wrong' way.

As you know, emotion is a physiological phenomenon; it is stimulated by your thoughts and the appraisal you make of a situation. When we vent and repeatedly tell others about a situation, we describe the 'right' appraisal we made and the 'right' emotions and feelings we experienced. But if we vent with people who won't challenge our assessment of a situation, we may never find out that our appraisal and emotional reactions were, in fact, inappropriate. Venting the wrong way trains your body to be over-sensitive to 'bad' experiences and keeps us focused on negativity longer. It doesn't resolve the underlying causes of your problems, particularly when you are venting to a caring friend, not a trained professional.

Simply repeating our description of a situation to others makes our body and mind relive that situation again and again. Those unpleasant and unhappy feelings are repeated and therefore more firmly entrenched. The more you vent this way, the more you put your body in the stress-reactive mode and the more you're acutely attuned to the traces that make you feel bad and then react automatically. Since your brain is now primed to register those traces as stressors, it is more challenging for you to pause and re-assess the situation objectively and choose your reactions wisely.

Venting in this way can be like scratching a mosquito bite. It feels like it works at first, but later that bite itches even more and you are trapped in a never-ending vicious loop.

BENEFITS OF UPGRADING YOUR EOS

Well, let's be honest here.

You started a business because you are smart, diligent, and have know-how in your chosen industry. These are all the qualities you need to get you started, but are they enough for you to survive and thrive?

The answer is NOOOOO!

Great business is always about people, and great companies are made up of great teams. Regardless of the industry you are in, your business is a people business, and people are emotional animals! Understanding emotion and leveraging emotions are critical to your business.

Being your own boss starts from the ownership of your emotions. If your EOS is constantly defaulting to the settings described earlier, you won't be functioning optimally. But if you upgrade your EOS, the benefits will flow through your business.

Improved productivity and performance

In the business world, we have long believed that people should leave their emotions at the door, and we should always keep a clear line between emotions and the work in hand.

The problem is, this is not really possible, and doesn't improve performance or productivity as expected. Humans are emotional beings; we constantly express our emotions, whether we are mindfully aware of it or not. Emotion shows up in our body language, our word choice, tone of voice, and our actions. It's part of who we are!

Researchers at Atlassian set out to understand how eight core emotions – anger, fear, disgust, surprise, sadness, trust, anticipation and joy – are expressed at work and what their relationship with productivity is. They found that **emotions that are expressed, addressed and resolved** will positively contribute to performance and team productivity.[12]

Researchers Stein and Book report that '... *studies have shown that [IQ] can serve to predict between 1% and 20% (the average is 6%) of success in a given job. EQ [or EI], on the other hand, has been found to be directly responsible for between 27% and 45% of job success ...*'.[13] And that percentage is even higher for those in leadership positions!

Quoted by Maaheem Akhtar in his blog 'Developing Emotional Intelligence Skills for High Performance Cultures', an annual survey conducted by the APA (American Psychological Association) in 2007 found that *'90% of the top performers have a high EQ. Additionally, they make $29,000 more annually than their low EQ counterparts.'*

High performers are able to combine intellectual ability with high and balanced elements of emotional intelligence when they perform! You can't argue with findings like that. It's clear that an upgraded EOS is going to be good for business.

More engaging and effective leadership

So, we've established that you can't keep emotions out of the workplace, but you do have to be careful about how you express them. The key for you as a leader is composure.

Too often, business leaders appear to be the opposite of composed. They can come across as a tyrannical leader who micro-manages, expresses rage when things go wrong, and uses fear and blame for motivation. I know that you don't want to be perceived as a tyrant, but when leading a team through turmoil it can feel like that's the only option, because your subconscious thoughts and unregulated emotions work together to do crazy things. When you, as a leader, break down under pressure, your team's performance and morale will surely be impacted.

In 1995, Daniel Goleman popularised the concept of emotional intelligence and publicly stated that 'The most effective leaders all have the highest degree of emotional intelligence.' Leaders with the highest degree of EQ are usually considered to be leaders with a high level of composure. This means they are calm, even in the heat of the moment. They are in control of their mind and emotions and impulses, and perceived by others as certain and confident.

I'm not saying you should never show your vulnerability. I am saying that being authentic, controlling your impulses and remaining level-headed under pressure is a skill that you can train and grow. This will allow you to stay open-minded and curious in highly stressful situations. In turn, this earns you the respect and trust of your people. When you behave in a composed manner, your people will be confident that, even in an unpleasant situation and when you are not pleased, you won't project your strong emotions onto them and you won't belittle them or be rude. They will know that you have their backs.

HOW TO UPGRADE YOUR EOS

Upgrading your EOS follows the same process as upgrading your other operating systems. First you need to identify your personal default settings. Then, you need to plug in a new set of beliefs. And finally, you need to adopt some key practices to ensure your EOS is operating at its best.

STEP 1: RECOGNISE YOUR DEFAULT SETTINGS

Before making any improvement in your EOS, we need to identify the default settings of your system and the errors it's producing. Earlier we talked about common default settings among business leaders, and now I'd like to give you a couple of tools to identify yours.

Tool 1: Track your mood and habits with Daylio Journal
Daylio Journal is a paid app, available on iOS and Android, that helps to track your mood, activities, goals and habits. If you are not a big fan of journaling but curious about how your daily activities affect your mood, Daylio can be a great alternative. You can log your moods, activities, habits and goals daily, including your sleeping routines, your diet and other health habits.

It is very easy to use, and is designed to present you with

insights, data and statistics in a user-friendly and easy-to-understand manner. If you are curious about your mood, Daylio could be a good start.

Tool 2: Thought-emotion recorder

If you are more serious about understanding your emotions, the thought-emotion recorder could be a useful tool.

As you already know, thoughts and emotions are intertwined. The thought-emotion recorder will help you identify the thought patterns that trigger emotions.

Recording your thoughts and emotions is a powerful tool to get in touch with your feelings.

This type of journaling is a way to identify your feelings and the actions taken around them. This tool will help you trace and monitor your feelings, and if you stick to it and use it correctly, you can begin to get around your own defences.

Here is a simple example of a thought-emotion record.

Date	11/08/2022	
Situation **(What happened?)**	I texted my team leader Jane at 8pm for urgent work, but she didn't respond.	
Automatic thoughts **(What thoughts came into your mind?** **How strongly do you believe each** **thought? Rate your belief from 1-100.)**	She is ghosting me.	100
	What's wrong? Is she thinking of leaving the company?	90
Emotions **(What emotions do you feel? Rate the** **intensity of each emotion from 1-100.)**	Angry	100
	Anxious	100

The best time to use the thought-emotion recorder is when, after something (significant or not) happens, you notice some thoughts in your mind or changes in your feelings. Regardless of what your thoughts are, it's beneficial to write them down immediately, together with your feelings. You can also add a column to record bodily sensations when you become more practiced at using the recorder. Let's take the same example further.

Situation (What happened?)	I texted my manager Jane at 8pm for urgent work, but she didn't respond.	
Automatic thoughts (What thoughts came into your mind? How strongly do you believe each thought? Rate your belief from 1-100.)	She is ghosting me.	100
	What's wrong? Is she thinking of leaving the company?	80
Emotions (What emotions do you feel? Rate the intensity of each emotion from 1-100.)	Angry	100
	Anxious	100
Bodily sensations (What do you feel in your body?)	Heartbeat – faster Breath – short & shallow Stomach – tight, knotted Arms – tickling Legs – heavy Chest area – throbbing Skin around chest – warm	
Actions/behaviours exhibited on the spot. (What did you do?)	Pacing Called my assistant to find Jane Kept calling and texting Jane until she answered at 9pm	

If you record your feelings over several days or weeks, you will be able to see your patterns, gain more and more clarity about the automatic thoughts going through your mind, become more aware of the sensations experienced in your body, and be able to name your emotions more accurately. Together, all of this information provides you with a clearer view about the interconnections between your thoughts and emotions.

For example:

- Do you notice emotions in your body, or do you feel disconnected from your body?
- Can you find the right term to describe those emotions, or is your emotion-related vocabulary quite limited?
- Were the actions you took effective? Did they make the situation better or worse?

After you've been keeping the record for a while, refer to the default settings discussed earlier to see if you recognise any of these patterns in yourself.

STEP 2: PLUG IN NEW BELIEFS

Now that you have taken steps to reveal the default settings of your EOS, it's time to start upgrading them. As with your other operating systems, a key step is plugging in new beliefs to replace old, outmoded ones.

Belief 1: Emotions are neither good nor bad

Emotions are neither right nor wrong, good nor bad. They just are. Feelings are never right or wrong; they just are. It's only behaviours that can be right or wrong, good or bad.

Instead of judging your emotions as either 'good' or 'bad', try to think of them as messengers – as part of an internal navigation system that helps us tap into a rich source of knowing. Think of emotions as the message in a bottle bringing important information to the shore of your consciousness.

Emotions contain information about us and the people and world around us. They are indicators of habits, beliefs or instincts that we have, but which we may not be consciously aware of most of the time.

A dramatic demonstration of how emotions can act as important messengers – how they can tell us something that we may not be consciously aware of – comes from the Iowa Gambling Task. This experiment demonstrates the connection between physiology, emotion and decision making. It was first designed by Antoine Bechara and his colleagues in 1994, and has been duplicated widely since then.

Imagine you walk into a room and researchers show you four decks of cards: two decks in red and two decks in blue. You are asked to pick a card from either deck, one at a time. You're told that some cards will win you money, while some will cost you money. But you don't know which ones will do what.

The truth is, red decks are minefields, and you are more likely to lose money by picking cards from the red deck, and you can really only get ahead by picking cards from the blue deck. So, can you guess how many cards you need to turn over to discover this? Well, most people turn over forty or eighty cards before they realise what's happening.

But this is where the experiment gets interesting. The researchers hooked each participant up to a polygraph (commonly known as a 'lie detector'), which can detect sweat on our skin when we are nervous. What the Iowa scientists found was that the polygraph detected sweat on the participants' skin long before their behaviour began to change and they started favouring the blue decks! In fact, they generally began to sweat after turning over just ten cards. So, you can see how our bodies express emotions physiologically long before our conscious minds are aware of what is happening.

The participants had a physiological experience before they were consciously aware of it AND it affected their behaviour before they could make sense of it. That's interesting for you to consider – when and how are your decisions being affected by your emotional state? Are there times this is happening that you're not aware of? If you can stop judging your emotions as either good or bad and accept that they are messengers, you could heed their messages.

Emotional awareness simply means recognising, respecting and accepting your feelings as they happen. And, when they happen, acknowledging the information they carry.

Have you missed the messages that your emotions are trying to tell you?

Belief 2: Feeling a feeling and expressing emotion is a sign of strength

In business, we don't talk about feelings.

I still remember, more than ten years ago, when I proposed launching an emotional wellbeing program in the company I worked for. I was told 'NO! Definitely NOT!' as if talking about emotions would hurt corporate performance.

For too long, talking about feelings and emotions has been considered a sign of weakness in business. It is regarded as the fluffy stuff, that it's about whining, crying, bitching and moaning, and that expressing emotions in the office makes you a 'sensitive, needy' person or a 'sissy' if you are male. For too long the perception has been that if you want to be professional, you have to grow a 'thick skin' to hide your emotions. But hiding is never the right way of expressing yourself.

To look professional, we have been trained to believe that:

- If I allow myself to feel this emotion, I'll completely lose control.
- A strong person doesn't have emotions/fear.
- If I tell other people how I really feel, they will think I'm weak.

But these beliefs are wrong. Being able to express your emotions skilfully, whether they are positive or negative, actually helps you bond with others. It is a trait that makes you authentic, but it does require a lot of courage and skill.

As you already know, human beings are emotional animals. When we have similar emotional experiences, we feel close to each other; when we experience similar emotions at the same time, we bond emotionally.

However, if we haven't learnt how to express emotions skilfully as we were growing up, it's likely that we won't feel comfortable when we experience them. When I grew up, the only emotion my parents felt comfortable expressing was anger. It was okay for them to raise their voices, but it was super awkward for them to express gratitude and joy. It wasn't that they didn't experience gratitude and joy – it was just that they found it challenging to verbalise those feelings. I remember that Mum used to express her happiness in a lowered voice, almost like a whisper, as if expressing happiness and gratitude was wrong and the moment you said it out loud it would evaporate.

When you accept that expressing emotions and feelings is an act of courage and strength, you open the door to learn how to express them skilfully. You can express your emotions by discussing them, writing about them, redirecting them to the right people, or even by ruthlessly pummelling a poor punching bag.

I once worked in a super stressful environment, and the one thing that carried me through that difficult time was a dart board that my boss hung in my office. He put his picture on it and said, 'Feel free to throw darts at me whenever you think I've pushed you too hard, but we have to get through this project.' Bang! I threw a LOT of darts at his picture!

STEP 3: EMPLOY NEW PRACTICES

Now that you have taken some time to identify the default settings of your EOS and learnt about new beliefs to plug in to begin the upgrading process, it's time to look at the practices you can use on an ongoing basis to ensure your EOS is in good shape.

Practice 1: Cultivate positivity

For evolutionary reasons related to our survival, our brains tend to have more negative thoughts than positive ones, we tend to focus more on negativities, and we pay more attention to negative events. We often say that 'failure is the mother of success' because we tend to learn more from failure.

Loretta Breuning, PhD, founder of the Inner Mammal Institute, puts it like this in her book, *Habits of a Happy Brain*:

> *'Our brain is not designed to create happiness, as much as we wish it were so. Our brain evolved to promote survival. It saves the happy chemicals (dopamine, serotonin*

and oxytocin) for opportunities to meet a survival need, and only releases them in short spurts which are quickly metabolised. This motivates us to keep taking steps that stimulate our happy chemicals ... You can end up with a lot of unhappy chemicals in your quest to stimulate the happy ones, especially near the end of a stressful workday.' [14]

You see, our brain is not designed to make us happy. It is designed to keep us safe so that we can survive a harsh environment. But in this modern era, our living conditions are relatively safe. And our survival-focused brain creates some conflict in us. As Dr. Breuning says:

'The bad feeling of cortisol has its own survival purpose. It alerts you to an obstacle on the path to meeting your needs so you can navigate your way to good feelings. But once you do that, your brain finds the next obstacle. You will feel bad a lot if you follow your survival brain wherever it leads.' [15]

So, we need to train ourselves away from this natural tendency. Upgrading your EOS is about retraining your emotional brain to notice and cultivate positivity, so that we can create a balance. We need to notice the good in the bad and rewire the brain to identify positivity among the negatives.

One practice I have been following was created by Rick Hanson, the author of *Buddha's Brain* and one of my favourite psychologists. He believes we can train our body to cultivate positive emotions.

Rick believes one of the best ways to develop happiness and other inner strengths is to focus on experiencing positive moments and then instilling them (remembering them, savouring them, turning them over and over in your mind). And slowly, these good mental states will become neural traits.

His four-step **HEAL** process is quite simple, but makes sense:

- **Step 1: Have a positive experience.** This is about the simple pleasures in life – the brief, positive experiences that occur in everyday settings and are accessible to most people at little or no cost. Examples include taking a walk in the sun, having a cup of tea, or finding a parking spot on a busy street. These experiences can be different for different people; what matters is that these simple pleasures bring you joy and happiness.

- **Step 2: Enrich the experience** by mindfully attending to it. Take ten or twenty seconds to take in the experience. This is also known as 'savouring the moment'. In psychology, savouring the moment is about intentionally focusing your attention on the positive side of the experience. You pause, block out distractions, and pay close attention to subtle sensations, your perceptions, your inner voice and your feelings at that moment. You simply allow yourself the time to thoroughly enjoy that momentary pleasure.

- **Step 3: Absorb it** by imagining all parts of your body are taking in that positivity. Feel that sense of pleasure flowing inside you through every fibre of your nerves and to every cell. Imagine they are all singing with joy, and you are the conductor of this pleasant symphony. The more you play it, the more you can remember it.

- **Step 4 (optional): Link** this positive experience to negative material in order to soothe and even replace it. This might sound confusing, but in my view, it is actually the most valu-able step. Let me explain...

Let's be honest. Regardless of how much we cherish positive emotions, they won't be the only emotions we experience in life. Although it is necessary for us to pay attention to positivity, it would be wrong for us to ignore negative material in the back-ground – no matter how tiny it might be. Positivity and negativity can co-exist, and the more we are aware of this the more we can practise putting the positives in the foreground. This helps us to fight off the tendency to only focus on the negativities, and the more we make room for both, the more the positive feelings begin to disarm the negatives.

Let me give you an example. While I was writing this book, I had the opportunity to join a group of inspiring ladies for a seven-day hike on the Cape to Cape in Western Australia, which is the longest coastal track in the country at 125 kilometres. Before the trip, I had been a weekend day-hiker – walking around twenty kilometres a day, so it was a huge leap for me to hike almost twenty kilometres every day for seven days straight.

Every morning before starting the hike we met for breakfast, and I could sense my mixed feelings. On one hand, I was excited to start the day because another leg on the track meant breathtaking views that put me in awe of the power and magic of nature. But on the other hand, my feet were hurting, and I could feel the soreness in the back of my knees. I couldn't help wondering how soon this soreness would turn into pain and make every step unbearable. On another hand, I also knew my teammates would support me and wouldn't let me struggle on my own. Their small gestures of kindness, such as waiting for me to catch up to them, walking at a slower pace or holding my hands when my legs turned to jelly, always warmed my heart. And on another hand, the thought that I might be a burden for the team also created a sense of guilt.

Because I had been practising HEAL for so long, I learnt not to dwell on those negative factors, like my painful feet or the feeling of being the burden. Instead, I chose to enhance the positive experiences of the day. I cooked up my favourite Aussie breaky – fried eggs, mushrooms, spinach, cherry tomatoes and avocado – for myself and a few of the teammates. With several of us sitting together with plates full of colourful, delicious food, I took the time to let my body remember this moment – the warm, soothing, joyful feelings coming from both my companions and the food. Of course, my foot was still sore and I could feel the pain in the background, but my heart and mind were full of joy, appreciation and excitement. My mood was not overly clouded by those negative factors, and my memories of this hike are positive – although I still remember the pain in my feet.

Research backs up this idea that simple pleasures have the power to restore feelings of positivity and happiness, giving people the energy and perspective they need to pursue the difficult but important things in life.

The more we practise cultivating positive emotions, the more possible it is for us to be authentically grateful.

Practice 2: Recognise and regulate challenging emotions

Upgrading your EOS is all about recognising your emotions, and then learning how to regulate and utilise them for your own benefit. People with an upgraded EOS do much better at managing challenging relationships and dealing with difficulties and setbacks.

Emotion carries tremendous information that helps us to

understand a situation as well as our values, needs and wants. In turn, this assists us to make choices in alignment with who we want to be. Let's look at some specific ways of recognising challenging emotions that will also help you to put those emotions into perspective.

Turn towards the emotion

The key here is to shift your attention inwards. Instead of focusing on how the people or situation outside you made you feel, turn inwardly to notice where and how you experience this emotion. Physical sensations are often useful antidotes to strong emotional distress. When we tune in to our bodies, it can help us work through and express our emotions in a way that's constructive and healthy.

Allow time and space to pay attention to your emotion when it arises. In which part of your body do you feel it most vividly? Do you also notice its temperature, its tension? Does it move around in your body? How does it move?

The next step is to try to understand your feelings. You do this by looking at the story behind them. When we have strong feelings, we often create stories in our minds to explain them. It's the story, rather than the event, that leaves us feeling hurt, angry, and so on.

In Leo's case, the story he made up was that when people came to meetings five minutes late or when they submitted a less than perfect design, it meant they didn't care about the business, that they were undermining the business and it would collapse after losing clients' trust. But was this true?

After you identify your story, ask yourself:

- 'Do I know for a fact that my story is true?'

Most of the time, the answer to this question is: 'No, I don't know this to be true.'

In Leo's case, he needed to ask whether he was absolutely sure that his colleague was coming late on purpose or submitting a less than perfect design on purpose, because they don't care about the business, and so on.

Then, ask yourself one more question:

- 'If I didn't have this story, what would I think? What would I do?'

Questions such as these allow us to look at the situation in a more detached, objective way that frees us from our habitual negative interpretations. The answer to this question will reveal to us the most reasonable course of action.

Accurately label the emotion

If you are experiencing a strong emotion – positive or negative – you often find deeper emotions buried beneath the more obvious ones. For example, you may experience all the sensations relevant to anger, but instead of using the word 'angry' to label the emotion, take time to dig a bit deeper. Is it truly just 'anger', or does it also feel like 'irritation', 'stress', or 'frustration'? Get into the habit of finding two or three more words to describe strong emotions.

It is also important to understand the extremity of basic descriptors like 'angry' or 'stressed'. Every emotion comes in a variety of flavours. When you describe your emotion as anger, it's possible that you're just annoyed or feeling impatient. If you can describe your emotions more accurately, others can respond to your emotions accurately. And if you use extreme descriptions such as 'angry' when you are simply 'annoyed', you may well find that your emotions escalate to match that exaggerated description.

Write it out

Susan David, the founder of the Harvard/McLean Institute of Coaching and author of the number one *Wall Street Journal* bestseller *Emotional Agility*, once explained that:

> '...people who write about emotionally charged episodes experience an increase in their physical and mental well-being. The process of writing allows people to gain a new perspective on their emotions and to understand them and their implications more clearly.' [16]

So, this is what you can do:

Whenever you are experiencing a strong emotion, set a timer for twenty minutes to write about it. This exercise is different from traditional 'journaling'; writing your emotions out is more about processing your strong emotion.

When writing, write with an enquiring and curious attitude. Ask yourself:

- What truly triggered me? The behaviour? The word? The tone? The facial expression?
- Where does this trigger come from?
- What did I experience when I was triggered?
- What is my habitual reaction? What is my tendency when I feel I was triggered?
- When was the first time I reacted this way to deal with such a situation?

- Is this trigger still important for me?
- Is my way of reacting still useful for me?
- If I do get triggered again, what could I do differently?
- If I don't want to be triggered again, what do I need to do? What kind of boundaries shall I set up?

Write it out, and have a dialogue with yourself in your journal to investigate and discover the root of your emotions. Take this writing as an opportunity to build an intimate relationship with your emotions.

By doing so, the chances are you can be more sensitive to others' emotions as well, and that is the foundation for empathy, a critical quality for inspiring leaders.

Use different lenses

The emotions we experience are not reality, but the way we interpret reality.

That's all very well when things are going fine, but when you are caught up with strong emotions, it can be difficult to shift your perspective. This is when playing with different lenses can be helpful. To get over the strong emotions and get into the reality, you can shift the lenses you are using to perceive and interpret the reality.

You may notice that as soon as you shift the lenses to look at a situation from different angles, you activate your prefrontal cortex and put it to work. This defuses the limbic system, deactivating the amygdala.

Here are some alternative lenses you can use when you are challenged with strong emotions.

Reverse view lens

If you are triggered by someone, and if you find yourself ruminating on a particular incident, use the 'reverse view lens' by pausing and asking yourself, '*What would the other person in this conflict say? And how might they be right?*'

When you are in conflict with others, what is truly in conflict are the **values, perspectives and priorities**, not the person. Adopting the reverse view lens enables us to review the situation from the other person's perspective, which creates the opportunity to discover what we have in common.

Forward view lens

When caught up with strong negative emotions, we tend to believe what we are experiencing now is permanent. Well, as you already know, this is not true.

So, it can be helpful to use a 'forward view lens' to look at the situation and ask, '*How am I likely to view this situation in six months?*' Be curious about what you may see through this lens.

Helicopter view lens

Again, when we are stuck in challenging situations, it can be difficult to understand why. This can lead to us getting trapped in a victim mindset. When you notice yourself repeatedly thinking how unfair a situation is, or how hurt and how disappointed you are, pause, step back and ask, '*How can I grow and learn from this situation?*'

At the end of the day, we learn and grow from the experiences we have. Discovering the lessons you are set to learn from the reality you are experiencing is the only purpose of these experiences. Ask yourself:

- *What is actually happening?*
- *How did I create this feeling?*
- *What is it trying to teach me?*

Practice 3: Own your emotional experiences

In other words, be emotionally responsible for your experiences.

Your emotions are a result of the way you interact with what is happening around you and within you. They are the result of your unique experience. Two people may experience the same external circumstances, but have different emotions and express those emotions differently. You have the power to decide how you would like to feel in a particular set of circumstances.

Much of the time when I work with a client to address workplace performance matters, there are underlying emotional issues that need to be addressed first. And most of the time, it is clear to me that a person's poor performance or stress is associated with how others, such as a boss or a co-worker, express their emotions at work. It's as if our performance or behaviours are the by-default outputs of others.

As a leader, have you ever had a performance conversation with an employee who under-delivered but kept saying, 'So and so didn't provide data/reports/feedback ... to my work, which made me feel bad/ignored/under-valued ... so I couldn't deliver what you asked.' It's as if their poor performance is the default outcome of others not providing what they need at the necessary time. Unfortunately, I have witnessed way too many arguments about this between managers and employees.

If this is the norm in your business, as the leader, the time has come for you to role-model being emotionally responsible, which means taking responsibility for how you feel. Let's consider some examples:

When you notice that you are triggered by your employee's behaviour, instead of saying, 'You made me feel bad when you did that,' you could model being emotionally responsible by saying, *'When you did that, something inside me was triggered, which impaired my performance. I will spend time understanding what it is and where it comes from, so I won't be triggered next time, and my performance won't be negatively impacted.'*

Most importantly, stop blaming others for your feelings. Eliminate myth-based emotional labels from your vocabulary. Stop saying such things as, 'You really hurt my feelings,' or 'Sorry for hurting your feelings.' Instead, express your feelings in a non-judgemental way by articulating your feeling and your intention, and also suggesting solutions:

I feel ___ when you ____, because____, so could you please _____ so that _____?

Next time your employee complains that your lack of response makes them feel bad, try to guide them to articulate their feeling in a more self-responsible way. Instead of saying, 'Your lack of response made me feel under-valued and demotivated,' help them to learn to say, *'I feel under-valued because I want to incorporate your feedback in this proposal and chasing you for your input distracted me from my work right now. Could you please drop me a line and let me know your feedback by (when), so that I can incorporate your thoughts in the proposal by the end of this week?'*

The behaviour of other people may trigger your internal emotional process, but what you do about it is in your control.

Practice 4: Insert a space between stimulus and response

In his classic book, *Man's Search for Meaning*, Viktor Frankl wrote, *'When we can no longer change a situation, we are challenged to change ourselves... Everything can be taken from a human but one thing: the last of the human freedoms — to choose one's attitude in any given set of circumstances, to choose one's own way.'*

In the space between a stimulus and our response sits our true power and freedom to make choices. The moment we pause and claim this power to make a conscious choice, we are able to respond to a situation instead of being carried away by it. The worst way to express an emotion is to react to it – that is, lash out as if there is no space in between the stimulus and our response.

To find the freedom to choose between stimulus and response, it helps to be aware of what's happening as it's happening and not be disengaged and running on autopilot. So how do you do this? You need to learn how to insert a space between a stimulus and your response to it. Let me share some tips with you...

Take three breaths

This simple yet useful practice, which is part of Google's Search Inside Yourself (SIY) training, will help you to get off autopilot, refresh, be more present and make a *choice* about what to do next. When you find yourself in a situation and notice that something inside you has been triggered, take three breaths and follow this process:

- On the first breath, bring your attention to the process of breathing and notice how your body reacts to it.
- On the second breath, try to relax your body.

- On the third breath, ask yourself quietly: what is most important now?

At the end of these three breaths, you might be able to find an appropriate way to express your feelings.

Wait ninety seconds

This is an exercise suggested by Harvard neuroscientist Jill Bolte Taylor in her book *My Stroke of Insight*. She explains how we can use ninety seconds to regulate our emotional-neurological process.

> 'When a person has a reaction to something in their environment, there's a 90-second chemical process that happens; any remaining emotional response is just the person choosing to stay in that emotional loop...
>
> When something happens in the external world, chemicals are flushed through your body which puts it on full alert. For those chemicals to totally flush out of the body, it takes less than 90 seconds. This means that for 90 seconds you can watch the process happening, you can feel it happening, and then you can watch it go away...
>
> After that, if you continue to feel fear, anger, and so on, you need to look at the thoughts that you're thinking that are re-stimulating the circuitry that is resulting in you having this physiological reaction, over and over again.'[17]

The moment you start to take full responsibility for your emotions is the moment you start to realise that no one except you has the power to make you feel sad or angry. On a biological level, all emotions are actually the hormones flowing inside your body.

So pause, wait ninety seconds, and take back your power.

Articulate emotion as an experience, not an identity

For many of us, when we experience strong emotions, we tend to say, 'I am angry!' as if *you are* the anger. But you are not!

As you already know, what you feel in your body is the flow of a bunch of hormones that are triggered by a certain stimulus. *You* are not the anger – you are simply experiencing anger in your body. 'I am experiencing anger now,' is a more accurate expression. When you articulate emotion in this way, you're acknowledging its presence while simultaneously empowering yourself to remain detached from it. And when you are detached from it, it is easier to find the space to choose your response.

Practice 5: Talk it out

The practices we've talked about so far involve you working alone. But it's always nice to have a little help from our friends! We have to be careful here though, as sometimes our friends can unintentionally make things worse by agreeing with our position regardless of whether it's a healthy position. So let's look at the right way to go about 'talking out' our emotions.

We talked about venting earlier and discussed how it is a natural response to strong negative emotions, but it is also a response that can, in the long run, do more harm than good. The key is to learn how to vent the right way. So how do you do that?

Vent with qualified advisors

It's not always a good idea to vent with a caring friend, who tends to protect your feelings, who doesn't want you to feel bad, who tends to comfort you by saying '*Yes, you're right. It was those awful other people who made you feel this way and they are absolutely wrong.*

Instead, think of somebody you trust who can actually help you to process and grow from the experience. Who can help you see your blind spots, who is capable of showing you alternative perspectives, or who can help you identify your thinking-feeling patterns?

Do vent, but be selective about whom you vent to. If you need to process your strong emotions, don't just go to anyone. Instead, go to someone who genuinely wants to support you, but also has the skills to help you. Someone who won't judge you, criticise you, or impose their views and perspective upon you. Someone who won't put you down or invalidate your feelings, but can also help you to grow from this emotional experience. Someone needs to be your 'qualified advisor'.

To be your 'qualified advisor', a person must meet these criteria:

- They have your best interests at heart;
- They are willing to listen to you;
- They have the skills to support you (you will know this because, after the conversation, your mind is opened up, your head is turned, you heart is full of light and hope, and you know what to do next);
- They help you to expand and, most importantly;
- They don't impose their views or beliefs on you, but they inspire you to think and choose differently.

Such people can be hard to find, but if you are determined to find them, you shall find them.

Vent in your journal

Allow me to emphasise this one more time: writing is the best method for processing our thoughts and feelings. It is also the best way to understand ourselves deeply.

If venting is your habit, once you realise that you are venting, pull out your journal and pour out all your negative or overwhelming thoughts and emotions into it. You can express yourself in words, or you can draw – whatever you feel like. Just spill it out into your journal.

When you vent in your journal, feel free to whine, moan, groan and complain. Don't think you have to be positive or solution focused at that moment. Just write down your thoughts and emotions, ugly or petty. You don't need to impress anyone when you write in your journal, so write to yourself and be honest with yourself – your journal is the most caring listener you can find, so spill it all out! The more you vent in your journal, the more you are saving your positive self for the outside world. Even when you are blessed with caring friends, it is not necessary to treat them as our emotional rubbish bins 24/7.

When you vent in your journal, chances are you will be able to see your thinking-feeling-doing pattens. Do you see how you jump to conclusions or make assumptions? Do you see that you used a lot of 'shoulds' on others or yourself? Do you see your behavioural tendencies when you are caught up by strong emotions?

Practice 6: Embody equanimity

Equanimity is a concept from Buddhism. However, you don't have to become a Buddhist to attain equanimity. You can gain the benefits it offers by practising **noticing without reacting.** For example:

- **Noticing and accepting all feelings and thoughts**

    This is about simply noticing the feelings and thoughts that come to you, recognising them and allowing yourself to feel them. It's about not judging them, questioning them, arguing with them, suppressing them or ignoring them.

- **Staying in balance**

    When I think about staying in balance emotionally, I think about standing on the platform of Central Station, the biggest train station in Sydney, where hundreds of trains come and go and take you to pretty much anywhere in Australia.

    Staying in balance is like standing at the platform, watching the trains come and go without getting on one and letting it take me to places I don't want or plan to go. Just like the trains, you can also watch your emotions and thoughts come and go without letting them take you for a ride and transport them somewhere you don't want to be.

- **Remaining neutral to craving and aversion through all situations**

    You may have realised by now that the true causes of emotional turmoils are not the events, but the way we interpret them. Equanimity means staying non-attached to a situation. Stay neutral, remain on your platform, and watch the train of emotions and thoughts come and go. Allow whatever comes to you in that moment and feel whatever you feel in the moment without becoming attached to it or wishing it would go away. All situations, good or bad, are temporary.

    Of course, as humans we handle different situations

differently. Allow the time you need for processing your emotions, but try to maintain your equanimity. In other words, try not to attach yourself to the situation and let it swallow you. Keep your mind balanced and non-attached throughout the process.

What's next?

As a self-starter business leader, your passion is your key to success. It enables you to put your heart and soul into what you have committed yourself to, and provides you with non-stop self-determination to achieve whatever goal you set your sights on.

As a strong energy, passion drives you to move forward and conquer all the obstacles in your way, but it also creates trouble. As an emotion, it has to be managed so that your performance is not impaired.

Staying calm and composed when your emotions are triggered provides you the opportunity to gain access to the important information carried by your strong emotions, and allows you to consciously approach situations with thoughtful consideration. It might mean turning challenges into opportunities.

Upgrading your EOS and understanding your triggers will help you to stay calm and composed under pressure, and the pure action of being calm and composed speaks volumes about you as a leader and makes you a leader who is remembered positively.

Here is a simple self-assessment to understand the current state of your EOS.

Self-assessment: Emotional Operating System

The scale for each statement is 1–5.
1 = the statement does NOT resonate with me at all
5 = the statement describes exactly the way things are in my life

	1	2	3	4	5
1. I get out of bed in the morning feeling motivated to start the day.					
2. I tend to adjust my behaviour to what I think the situation calls for.					
3. I find it challenging to control my impulses.					
4. I rarely lose my temper under stress.					
5. I feel comfortable to be myself most of the time.					
6. I'm good at using emotion to motivate myself and others.					
7. I never allow a crisis to escalate into panic.					

My score is: _____

Chapter 4

Physical Operating System

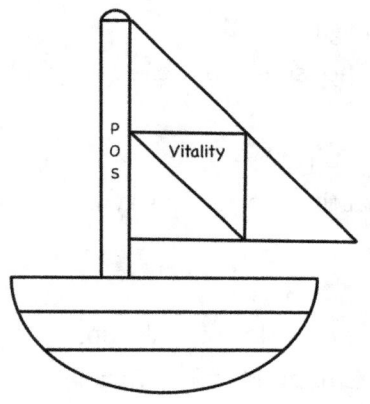

*Your heart can only take you so far – sometimes the
physical body tells you otherwise.*

— ABBY WAMBACH

Angela is a serial business owner. Over the past twenty
years, she has set up multiple businesses in various indus-
tries and countries, all of which had to close due to
problems with her physical health. When I met her, she
was slightly overweight and had constant stomach pain.
But she was also hard-working, and put her heart and soul

into the business she was running.

When I asked her: 'Can you describe your typical day?' she said, 'I start to work when I wake up.'

'Immediately?'

'Yes, when I'm still in bed I will check emails, and respond to the urgent ones.'

'Then?'

'Then I'll start to call employees while I'm washing my face or brushing my teeth.'

'And you choose to do these things at the same time because...?'

'Because I don't have time, and I don't want to be late.'

'Late? What time do you wash your face and brush your teeth?'

'8 a.m.'

'I see. What time do you wake up?'

'Usually 7 a.m., and it takes me an hour to read all the emails and messages.'

'I understand. And then?'

'Then I will start to work on the computer, and I'll be on the phone for the whole day'.

'Do you take breaks?'

'What do you mean "breaks"? I always have back-to-back meetings.'

'So, do you exercise?'

'Not much. I don't go to the gym, but if I can, I may walk the dog.'

'What time do you go to sleep?'

'It depends, but usually 2 a.m. or 3 a.m., as I can only sleep five or six hours, sometimes even less.'

'What do you do that late?'

'Working at night is quiet, and there's time for me to think. I have too many meetings and calls during the day, so night is the time I work on my stuff.'

'How's your energy level during the day?'

'Tired. That's why I don't exercise; I'm too tired to exercise.'

'How's your diet?'

'I like snacking. I may have one meal, like dinner, usually quite healthy, with veggies and meat, but during the day I snack on whatever is convenient – cookies or cakes or chips or coffee … anything I can find.'

Meet your engine

The physical operating system (**POS**) is in charge of your physical wellbeing, energy, stamina and resilience, and it affects and influences your mental strength. Your physical operating system is the engine of your inner world.

Your body is quite similar to a car, in a sense. Just as you need to take your car for a regular service and feed it with premium petrol for high performance, your body must also be maintained and nourished properly. Feeding it with rubbish food won't fuel it up for high performance, and a neglected and impaired physical operating system results in impaired performance.

But the POS doesn't operate on its own. Your mind and body are connected by your nervous systems – neural circuits made up of neurotransmitters, hormones and chemicals. Just like flawed thinking patterns can affect your body, your body also affects your mental performance. A poor lifestyle, which includes factors such as poor diet, insufficient sleep and lack of physical activities, results in a poor condition in your physical body. This in turn affects the performance of your brain. Your ability to focus, think clearly, and adopt and learn new ways of thinking and doing may go out the window.

Most leaders I meet through my work are knowledge workers, meaning they make a living through their 'smarts' and they credit their brilliant mind for all their success and achievements. But they tend to forget an important thing – that their 'smart' brain is part of their body, and their body is the engine that pumps up all their 'smartness'.

Most business leaders neglect this element of their lives because their business comes first. You put your heart and soul into your business, and like Angela you start to work the moment your eyes open and only allow yourself to stop work after the last drop of energy has been squeezed out of your body. Who has time for exercise?

But I believe physical and mental strength work together. The truth is, good physical health keeps your mind sharp and focused, and keeps you motivated. The best business leaders understand that preparing your body physically will not just help you defend against illnesses, but give you more stamina to last the long hours demanded by your busy lifestyle. You don't need to lift hundred kilo weights, but you do need to give your body the strength it needs to sustain performance.

So, if you rely on your 'smart' brain to earn the life you desire, it is time to understand how your POS works, because your brain is part of this system.

HOW YOUR POS WORKS

Of all our operating systems, the physical body is like the central piece that connects the mind, emotions and spirit. Physiologically speaking, the human body is made up of multiple interacting systems, and the purpose of these systems is to keep your body in balance.

Your respiratory system gathers oxygen and removes carbon dioxide; your muscular system allows the body to move; the digestive system breaks down food to release nutrients; the immune systems helps to detect and fight off disease ... all these systems interact with each other and affect each other. Among all the systems, the most important system that controls all the other systems is our nervous system.

In a nutshell, your nervous system comprises the central nervous system and the peripheral nervous system. The peripheral nervous system is made up of two parts: the somatic nervous system and the autonomic nervous system (ANS). The ANS is further subdivided into the sympathetic nervous system (SNS) and the parasympathetic nervous system (PNS).

The fight or flight state we discussed previously is managed by the SNS. Its job is to prepare the body to react to whatever happens in our environment. For example, if you walked into an overheated room, your SNS will make your body sweat a bit more so that you can cool down. If you walk down a dark street with no streetlights and you feel scared, the SNS will encourage your pupils to dilate so that your eyes can get more light in and enable you to see the surroundings a bit better. Your heartbeat might increase a bit, you may start to sweat, your muscles may tighten up and you may notice your hands make fists now. The SNS does all these things to prepare you either to fight off or run away from potential dangers.

On the other hand, when the PNS is activated, it relaxes your body, slows down your heartbeat, decreases your blood pressure and relaxes your muscles. Basically, it helps your body go back to a stress-free state. This is important to keep the body in balance. If the SNS is 'on' all the time, your body is constantly in this stress-reactive state, meaning the digestive system and the immune system will be shut down – you don't need these things to function when you're in a state of fight of flight.

The vagus nerve is the other important element of your nervous system. It is the longest nerve in the body and wanders from your brain all the way down to your gut. It connects all your vital organs and creates a two-way communication pathway between your brain and body. It also functions like a switch that turns the PNS and SNS on or off as needed. The stronger the vagus nerve, the more easily we can balance between our stress reactions and relaxation.

But of course, there is more to our POS than our nervous system. Our ability to do stuff – to walk, run, think, learn – all depends on the body's capacity to create energy via the food and drink we put into it. When food is broken down in your stomach, it is mixed with acids and enzymes, and sugars and starches in the food are turned into glucose – the type of sugar that provides immediate energy to the body.

Your brain needs a steady supply of fuel – glucose – for it to work, and glucose mainly comes from the food you eat. Although the brain only accounts for a tiny two per cent of our body weight, it consumes more than twenty per cent of the glucose-derived energy created by the body when it is idle.[18]

As a business leader, when you need to solve millions of problems a day, a sharp, well-functioning brain is your only secret weapon. When the glucose level in your bloodstream drops a little, your ability to pay focused attention, learn or memorise will be impaired. The more sufficient and steady the supply of glucose in your blood, the better you can deal with more complex or demanding mental tasks.

Your brain also needs a steady flow of oxygen to maximise its cognitive functions, and how much oxygen your body can use in a given time is determined by your level of cardio fitness. So you can see that your physical fitness is directly related to your mental fitness.

Your POS also makes you flexible. When you think of flexibility, you probably imagine stretching or doing yoga postures, rather than being flexible in your thoughts. But a flexible mind leads to a flexible body – and vice versa. Having a flexible mind indicates that you know what you want, but you are open to receiving new information and adjusting and adapting as required.

When the body is flexible, we can respond to stressors more fluidly. Imagine you're hiking a trail that requires you to climb up some rocks. A stiff body with a rigid mind would tell you, 'No, it is impossible!' And when you try to scramble up the rocks, all the tension accumulated in your joints will stop you from being able to move the way you need to. But if you have practised to make your body more flexible, it can redirect the tension to the areas of your body that you need to get you up those rocks. And your flexible mind will also tell you, 'It is possible – give it a try.' With a more flexible mind and body, both your business life and everyday living can be easier.

Your physical health also has a direct bearing on your emotional reactions, and one way this plays out is through the connection between your brain and your gut. The brain and gut communicate with each other through the microbiota-gut-brain axis. The vagus nerve is the interface of the gut-brain axis, and is the communication channel between these two elements.

To understand how this all works, consider how the pure thought of giving a speech on stage may cause your stomach to churn. And if you feel nervous about walking onto the stage, you may have to run for the bathroom more often. Excitement can directly impact your stomach and intestines. Your gut communicates with your brain as well, and when your gut or stomach is distressed you may also experience the emotions of stress, anxiety or depression.

This is just one more compelling reason to live a healthy lifestyle that includes exercise and a good diet.

DEFAULT SETTINGS OF THE POS

Since the day we were born, we began to grow and survive through trial and error. There is no ONE textbook or manual that we can use to pre-plan our life or business.

Most of the time, we develop our own maps by testing out what works and what doesn't. Along the way, we unintentionally develop habits and patterns and beliefs that were useful for us at certain stages but may not continue to fulfil our needs later on. This is true for all our operating systems, including our POS. In fact, not only do these habits, patterns and beliefs fail to fulfil our needs, they can seriously undermine our health, happiness and success. Let's look at some of the common default settings of the POS.

Unhealthy coping mechanisms

As young professionals working hard in demanding positions, sometimes we needed to soften the edges of pain. And what did we do? We drank alcohol to loosen up, ate ice-cream to experience pleasure, scrolled on our little screens, played games or watched videos for hours to relax.

We learnt from our peers, and even caring friends, to approach stress destructively. In my early days working in corporate, 'Let's catch up for a drink after work' was code for 'I've had a shitty day; let's drink and whine it off.'

And it continues. Our waking hours are full of challenges and problems that require our attention. Sometimes it seems like the only way to enjoy our brief breaks is to indulge in eating or sharing a bottle of wine with colleagues and partners ... to bond, to relax, to fall asleep.

But both over-eating and drinking alcohol harm brain function.

Terry Davidson, who is the Trone Family Eminent Scholar Chair in Neuroscience and Behaviour at American University in Washington, DC, published a study in 2016 pointing out that over-eating and constant consumption of high-calorie food may reduce the functionality of the hippocampus, the part of the brain related to memory, and cause memory loss.[19]

Alcohol does something similar. As soon as it gets into the blood, it begins to affect your brain by working at the cellular level and disrupting and suppressing the neurons and connections related to memory.

Even if you just drink one or two nights per week, the neural network in the prefrontal cortex will be negatively impacted. As you know, the prefrontal cortex is considered to be the 'CEO' of your brain, because it carries out the functions of analysing, planning and decision making. Alcohol can disrupt the connections between the neurons in this area, and consequently reduce our ability to manage behaviours.

The more we drink, the thinner the neocortex will get. Remember that the neocortex is the part of the brain that differentiates human beings from other species – it is the part of the brain that makes us human.

If over-eating comfort food and having a drink or two is your way to relax or socialise or feel pampered, you need to reconsider your habits. It requires courage to step back, assess ourselves, examine a situation objectively and honestly, and ask: 'Is my way of self-indulgence actually self-sabotaging?'

The self-indulgent man craves for all pleasant things ... and is led by his appetite to choose these at the cost of everything else.

— ARISTOTLE, THE *NICOMACHEAN ETHICS*

When running your own business, there is no safety net, and it feels like our success depends on our diligence. That makes it hard to take time out of the business to care for ourselves. And it's natural that in the early stages, we tend to be wobbly in finding the right way to care for and indulge ourselves in order to be successful.

When I meet passionate business leaders like Angela, I often see red flags that indicate self-sabotaging behavioural patterns are getting in the way of their success. Rather than external circumstances preventing them from reaching their goals, they are doing things that are stopping them from reaching goals.

When work gets busy, what do you do to care for yourself? Eat irregularly, eat in front of your computer, eat a huge amount of food that is convenient to get? Open a bottle in the middle of the night? Binge watch TV or play computer games day and night while not working?

When I first confronted Angela about the need to take care of herself, she found excuse after excuse as to why this wasn't possible.

Smart business leaders are good at justifying their conduct, so what you tend to do is talk yourself out of self-care and convince yourself that you don't need it right now or that you need to focus on work and 'enjoy life' instead.

Constant exhaustion

I often meet young business owners who are diligent and hard-working, who started their business from scratch with their own two hands. Often, they started their business in their twenties, and one of the patterns they built was to work so hard that they felt guilty if they took time out for leisure or relaxation. They feel they must push themselves to the limit and only stop working when their physical body cannot function anymore. This becomes the only way they can feel sure that they did their best and gave it their all.

And while a business owner might be able to sustain this in the short term, if it becomes a default, long-term habit, they could be in trouble. When they reach their thirties, they start to notice a drop in energy, then performance. Their physical body can no longer take the punishment they've been dishing out. And while some of them start to pay attention to the needs of their body, some just take it as a sign of the natural process of ageing. Well, ageing is a disease, in case you wondered.[20]

Each business that Angela set up lasted for about three to five years before her physical health collapsed and she had to close or sell the business. She then went into 'hibernation' for one or two or more years to get her strength back. With her physical system restored, she was once again driven by that never-satisfied entrepreneurial spirit and started a new business. And again, after three to five years, the stress and physical neglect caught up with her, her body collapsed again, and her latest business folded. It's not hard to see the pattern here.

If you love doing what you are doing, surely you want to know how your mind and body can work together to enable you to do what you love for longer. Upgrading your POS and cancelling damaging default settings will help you to keep doing what you love for longer and enjoy it more.

Workaholism

Workaholics were once hailed as 'heroes' of the corporate world for their commitment-at-all-cost attitude. But studies show that being addicted to work impacts negatively on productivity.

Many people confuse workaholism with high performance, but they're not the same thing.

The difference between the two is that workaholics do work to look important while high performers look for important work to do. Both workaholics and high performers are hard workers, and the way to tell the difference is to take a look at their working styles.

The corporate culture in Asia remains relatively inflexible and very much focused on sticking with a minimum thirty-eight-hour-plus work week, if not 996 (in other words, working from 9 a.m. to 9 p.m. for a minimum of six days per week), which has been common in the high-tech industry, but can also be found in most small businesses.

In this context, workaholics are unable to create boundaries. Competitive by nature, they are easily drawn into the notion that if they spend more time being busy, they will be rewarded for their relentless dedication. Workaholics choose work over everything else – forgoing time with friends and family, putting hobbies on hold and relinquishing relationships may be okay in the short term, but too often workaholics go for busyness, which means lots of work for little progress – as their personal life falls by the wayside. This is not a value-add strategy.

High performers, on the other hand, identify high-value tasks and get on with executing them efficiently. As Adam Grant nicely said:

*'Being a workaholic doesn't drive productivity. It's a recipe for languishing. Having fun isn't an enemy of efficiency. It's fuel for finding flow. Play isn't a reward for finally making it through your to-do list. It *belongs* on your to-do list.'*

Neglect

In our younger days, we believed that as long as we were alive, our body would be there to support us. A healthy physical body means keeping the doctor away. As long as a doctor is not involved, we are healthy enough to do whatever we need to do. But just as you regularly service your car to prevent wear and tear resulting in a major breakdown, so you should see your doctor or health practitioner for regular check-ups and maintenance.

Remember Leo – the driven executive running a digital marketing company, whose temper negatively impacted the business culture and performance? When we first met him, he was overweight but refused to exercise or control his diet. The more we dug into his situation, the more it was revealed that his short temper came from his impaired liver, which came from his lifestyle. The root cause of his business performance was not the attitude or competency of his team, but what he ate and drank, and how he treated his body. Had he found this problem earlier, it may not have escalated into such a large issue.

Running a business is a long game; it is a marathon with heaps of sprints. You might think that a doctor only needs to get involved when there is injury that will slow you down or stop you from continuing. But paying attention to your physical health before doctors are involved is more about maintenance and prevention – maintaining that high performance and preventing a possible downslide.

As you already know, and let's not forget, your brain is part of your physical body. If you want to outperform others on the track, working *with* your mind and body instead of working *against* them might be a wise choice.

BENEFITS OF UPGRADING YOUR POS

A fit body is like a smoothly running factory that produces fresh energy and resources for your mind to function.

The main purpose of upgrading your POS is to work with your brain and body, not against them.

Because...

You will be smarter and happier

A study conducted by James A. Mortimer and Yaakov Stern, and published in *Neurology* in 2019, followed 454 adults over twenty years and concluded that regular physical exercise is the most 'inexpensive and effective way to delay the onset of cognitive decline and dementia'.[21]

Why so?

When you exercise your body, it creates more energy that you can use to function or perform. Just ask those regular gym goers. They know that not exercising the body actually results in dips of energy, particularly after the age of thirty-five. For this very reason, I transformed myself from a couch potato in my twenties to a regular gym goer in my forties – a habit that took me almost twenty years to build.

When you exercise your body, it also helps your brain to increase its capacity and sharpen its focus for at least two to three hours afterwards. When more blood flows to your brain, more brain-derived neurotrophic factor (BDNF) is released. BDNF functions as fertiliser for your brain and helps to maintain the health of your brain cells and grow new cells.

Exercise also releases a flood of beneficial chemicals. For example, endorphins are released, which reduce your perception of pain and lead to positive feelings and a general sense of wellbeing. Serotonin is released, which makes you feel good and improves your mood, counteracting the effect of stress and anxiety. Have you ever noticed that after a long day at work, simply walking home will make you happier?

Wouldn't you be the smartest one when your mood, energy and brain all work in your favour?

If you met Leo today, you would notice that he is no longer overweight. At my last coaching session with him, he offered me a small bag of nuts instead of a sugary drink as he used to, and said, 'Well, I do notice the difference in my energy level and temper since I started to exercise and watch my diet.'

If you want to catch Angela today, you might find her walking in the park while conducting a video call. 'Exercise and a good night's sleep are non-negotiable for me now,' she told me. Remember – you can be as creative as you like to incorporate exercise in your busy schedule.

You will be a better leader

Research conducted by the Centre of Creative Leadership claims that 'executives who are physically fit are also considered to be more effective leaders than those who aren't.'

Why?

Because whatever you do to your body will directly impact your brain's ability to function, and hence improve your overall performance. A healthy lifestyle helps leaders better cope with the stresses and demands of their positions, ultimately increasing their leadership effectiveness.

Exercise boosts brain health and function in just about every way that we can measure. In tests that measure long-term memory, reasoning, attention, problem solving, creativity and fluid intelligence, research has consistently shown that exercisers outperform couch potatoes. It also makes you more resilient. As a business leader, you have to be able to face tough challenges every day while maintaining mental focus on your priorities.

The mental qualities required to undertake regular physical activity also have synergy with leadership. When I was in school, I would cry for death if I had to run 800 metres. I'm a couch potato by nature, and if you're like me, then you would understand that getting physically active requires discipline, setting goals and following them through. Transferring that skillset into business, it means a business leader can adopt a goal-focused approach and then relentlessly work towards realising the company's goals and helping their teams fulfil professional and personal life goals.

In today's very hectic lifestyle, being able to prioritise time to maintain a healthy lifestyle enhances your ability to set goals, plan ahead, give priority to what matters and, most importantly, work on minimising the negative effects of your inertia and keeping yourself accountable, which are the skills in high demand in the business world.

You will have greater self-mastery

Self-mastery is about the ability to recognise, understand, control and make the most out of your physical, mental, emotional and spiritual self. It revolves around the idea that leadership starts with you – that regardless of your title, your leadership starts from the inside out. Gaining self-mastery involves our intelligence regarding our physical body, as well as our mental, emotional and spiritual operating systems.

As the leader of your business, you are responsible for setting goals, as well as executing strategies and implementing solutions that will achieve those goals. This process might require working relentlessly to adjust, adapt and commit to doing things outside your comfort zone.

Paying attention to your body, understanding how your body functions, and establishing habits to enhance its performance instead of indulging in habits that may provide immediate pleasure but harm your performance in the long run, is difficult. You must make diligent and consistent efforts to discover your habits and tendencies, regulate your impulses, and replace poor habits with better ones.

It is important to realise that physical intelligence doesn't just sit alongside mental, emotional and spiritual intelligence; it under-pins them. It enhances cognitive function and influences one's ability to live a happy, fulfilled, successful life.

As a busy business leader, the first thing you learn to master is stress – our built-in psychological and physiological reaction to an event or condition that is considered to be a threat or challenge.

When your **Emotional Operating System** is upgraded, chances are you will be more skilful in terms of differentiating the source of the stress. When your **Mental Operating System** is upgraded, you will have the ability to shift your attention, and be more flexible in terms of managing your focus and what you pay attention to. When your **Spiritual Operating System** is upgraded, you are more closely connected with your big WHY and HOW. Together, all these systems contribute to turning 'bad' stress into 'good' stress. Finally, your upgraded **Physical Operating System** plays a vital role in noticing the stress that is building up in your body, and reminding you to re-design or re-orient your daily activities to minimise its negative impact on your body and mind.

HOW TO UPGRADE YOUR POS

Upgrading your physical operating system works the same way as upgrading your other operating systems. And by now you should know the drill – recognise your default settings using the tools provided, plug in a new set of beliefs, and then begin a new set of lifelong practices that will ensure your system remains upgraded in the future.

STEP 1: RECOGNISE YOUR DEFAULT SETTINGS

You may be familiar with that famous saying from the late Peter Drucker, the most influential thinker and educator on management: 'No measurement, no management.' We can apply that to our physical operating system. We have lived in the same body since the day we were born, but 'feeling' that it is running fine is no guarantee that it is. We need to understand its true state of operation.

Tool 1: Measure resilience with HRV

It's hard to get through an average day without hearing about resilience now. We tend to believe 'resilience' is something in our mindset, but the reality is that our ability to bounce back sits in our physical body as well!

Numerous researchers have suggested that heart rate variability (HRV) is a possible marker of resilience and behavioural flexibility. HRV measures your physiological resilience to stress by indicating how well you handle your emotions when faced with changes in the environment.

Unlike heart rate measurement, which measures the average number of heart beats per minute, HRV measures the temporal variation between each heartbeat. For example, it might be 0.8 of a second between two beats, or 1.1 seconds between another two beats.

The variations between heartbeats is controlled by the autonomic nervous system (ANS), and indicates the alterations of the two arms of the ANS – the sympathetic nervous system (SNS) and parasympathetic nervous systems (PNS). The SNS is the system that is activated under stressful situations – it's the source of the fight or flight response we discussed earlier. The PNS is the system that takes over when the threat has passed and returns the body to a healthy, stress-free state.

When the SNS is activated, the HRV reading tends to be lower, meaning the time between subsequent heartbeats tends to be shorter. When the PNS is activated, the HRV reading tends to be higher, meaning the time between subsequent heartbeats is longer.

If the activation ratio between these two nervous systems is about SNS:PNS = 6:4, this indicates that you manage your stress well, and your parasympathetic nervous system is strong enough to balance the stress your body experiences. This further suggests that people who have a high HRV may have greater cardiovascular fitness and may be more resilient to stress.

Monitoring HRV reveals the relationship between our daily activities and bodily reactions.

For some of my clients, cooking is relaxing while driving puts the body in high stress. For others, eating is relaxing while drinking coffee or watching news is stressful. But for almost all of us, having a glass of wine at night to relax causes our HRV to drop and our resting heart rate to rise. This means your body is in stress-reactive mode when you are trying to relax and recover – for example, while you are sleeping. Thinking that wine will help us to relax is a lie we tell ourselves.

If you monitor your HRV as you incorporate more mindfulness, meditation, sleep and, especially, physical activity into your life, you may find positive changes. For those who love data and numbers, this could be a great way to track how your nervous system is reacting not only to the environment, but also to your emotions, thoughts and feelings.

If you are serious about monitoring your daily HRV reading and changing your habits, then check out **Apple Watch Gen 7**, **Whoop**, and the **Oura ring**. And if you are into sports, **Polar** and **Garmin** both offer various data measurement to help understand your HRV and stress levels in your body.

Tool 2: Measure your fitness with VO2max

Vo2max measures how much oxygen you can absorb or use while exercising at a maximum level, hence the name: maximal volume (V) of oxygen (O2) your body can use during exercise. Your VO2max reading indicates how powerfully your heart and blood vessels can push blood to your muscles and the rest of your body. The higher the reading, the more oxygen you can breathe in and consume, and the more energy your body can create.

Your body is your engine, and to be able to create more energy for us to function we need a lot of oxygen. This means we need good lungs to take in as much oxygen as possible, and a strong heart and circulatory system to transfer the oxygen to muscles and other body parts for them to function. The fitter you get, the bigger your muscle mass becomes and the stronger your cardio system is, the better your body functions – and your body includes your brain.

A research paper published in 2017 suggested that 'higher aerobic fitness, as measured by VO2max, is associated with enhanced cognitive functioning'.[22] The higher your VO2max, the better your cardio fitness level, the better you are at learning and memorising information.

Without getting too technical, you can measure your VO2max with most smartphones with sports readings – for example, the **Apple Watch Series 3** or later. The **Garmin watch**, **Fitbit** or any other fitness tracker popular with runners and health-conscious people will also measure your VO2max.

Tool 3: Test your gut microbiome

The gut microbiome has attracted a lot of attention in recent years. There are about 300 to 1,000 species of bacteria in the gut, and each of them plays a different role. Together they create a dynamic ecosystem inside us, and this ecosystem has a direct impact on our overall health and wellbeing, affecting such things as sleep quality, stress response, anxiety and memory function.[23]

In recent years, it has become common knowledge that a healthy gut means a healthy brain, and a healthy gut is determined by what we feed those microbiomes. The more nutrients the food you eat has and the healthier and more diverse this gut ecosystem is, the better your food can be digested and the better your immune system is controlled. All this leads to better protection of your brain function.

To understand your unique gut ecosystem, you can do a gut microbiome test.

If you are in Australia, the **Microba Insight**™ kit is a good place to start. Microba launched its personal gut microbiome testing in Australia in 2018, and claims it is 'the most comprehensive microbiome test available'.

In 2019, I ordered my Microba Insight™ Sampling Kit. About three weeks after sending back the samples, my results landed in my inbox and I was sent to my online portal. It was quite fascinating to be introduced to the bacterial species living in my gut and understand their functions, such as their ability to break down protein or their potential to prevent kidney or cardio diseases, as well as suggestions for beneficial changes.

Why not give it a try?

STEP 2: PLUG IN NEW BELIEFS

The next step in upgrading your POS is – you guessed it – to plug in new beliefs!

Belief 1: Constant exhaustion is a mark of stupidity, not diligence

When I first read this line from *It Doesn't Have to Be Crazy*, written by Basecamp founders Jason Fried and David Heinemeier Hansson, I laughed. A blunt truth told by financially successful business owners made it more convincing, right?

In the business world, sometimes we need a nudge to realise that it is not necessarily the hours we put in that makes work more productive. It is more about wasting less time, having fewer distractions and experiencing less man-made stress and anxiety ... which leaves you enough time to focus on working on what truly matters.

Instead of pushing your body to keep working at all costs, train yourself to work smartly!

When I asked Angela about her team, this was how she described her people:

> 'Brendon is great. If I asked him to do a report, he would send it to me at 3 a.m., and I believe he is really passionate about the work. Rebecca is different. She has a young family and she is quite occupied outside of working hours, and I have told her that I'd like to see more passion from her.'

In my early days in corporate, I was that passionate, perfectionist, driven employee who was proud of running more than 100 miles a day, every day. I literally chose to run to the bathroom and meeting rooms, because there was so much to do and I didn't want to waste a second. I only closed my computer late at night when the last drop of energy in my body was dried up. And some of my most enjoyable times at work were when we were chasing a deadline or trying to remedy a complex problem under high pressure.

While on the one hand it did make me feel that I had given my best, on the other hand it also drained my adrenals and led to a low cortisol state. I experienced adrenal depletion firsthand, which comes with brain fog, low energy, depressed mood, and salt and sweet cravings. Oh man, I used to have a drawer packed with lollies in the office, and every single day I had to have a bag of sweets to pick me up at 3 p.m.

Contrary to what we used to believe, functioning this way doesn't guarantee sustained high performance. In fact, uncontrolled 'passion' can backfire and burn us up.

The inverted U theory that Yerkes and Dodson created in the early 1900s has proved it. This theory describes a clear relationship between pressure and performance. It indicates that once the stress level becomes more than moderate, performance drops significantly, and pushing the body without proper self-care usually results in exhaustion and burnout.

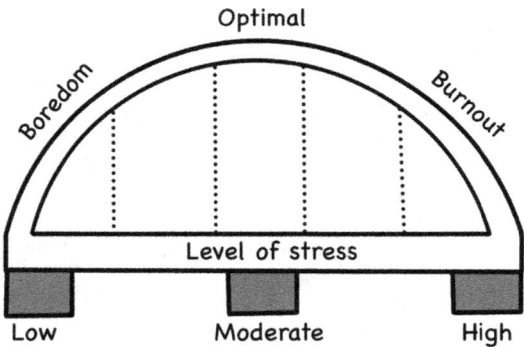

If you want to achieve high performance sustainably, constantly pushing your body to the extent of exhaustion is not a wise approach.

You need to change the way you think about this and replace

the old thinking with a new belief – one that is supported by science, and the understanding that constant exhaustion is nothing more than stupidity.

Belief 2: Slowing down is the best way to speed up

We tend to confuse 'fast' with 'efficient and better'. As if engaging in quick actions and moving as fast as possible from A to B in a controlled and straight line is the perfect approach. In reality, usually the opposite is true. If sustained high performance is your goal, then speeding up isn't the answer. It often makes things more complex, consumes more energy and, even in the best case, solves only a part of the challenge.

But when you slow down, you can eventually go deeper and faster into achieving your objectives. You can deal more effectively with increased complexity and challenges – and use less energy. The slow-down-to-speed-up strategy creates a process that requires you to pause at key moments in the decision-making process, review data, and include other perspectives before finalising an important decision.

The same applies to your physical body.

The state of your physical body has a direct impact on your mental ability, but you don't have to drag your body on a 100-mile run every day. It won't hurt to schedule some downtime in your diary on a quiet Wednesday afternoon so that you can leave work a couple of hours early. There's nothing wrong with taking a 'disconnected' weekend, when all work-related emails and messages simply cannot be delivered to you. It also means taking a nap in the afternoon, even on a busy day, or creating a 'winding down' routine at night to get a restful sleep. These things allow you to renew your physical energy.

And when it comes to exercising the body, short but regular bouts of exercise are more beneficial than long, irregular ones. Slowing down can help you to speed up. The very first lesson I learnt from my running coach was: run slowly! Listen to your body – speed is not the only measure for long-lasting success.

Belief 3: You can trust your gut

Scientifically speaking, your head, heart and gut are connected. Each of them has tremendous numbers of neurons and they communicate with each other via the vagus nerve. They work together to control how we think, feel and act. Hence, it is said, we don't just have one brain. We have three.

But these three elements don't always work well together. Your heart might desire one thing, but your logical and analytical mind might try to convince you to go in another direction, or your physical body will simply fail to provide the energy and strength needed.

This new belief is about embracing the role your body plays in helping you function as a leader. It's true that you can both 'trust your gut' and 'follow your heart' in business. Of course, I'm not saying your mind is always wrong, but as we've seen in earlier chapters, because its role is to protect you and stop you from getting closer to possible dangers, it can be over-protective sometimes.

So let your heart and gut be your wiser advisors here and believe that they play a role for you. Don't ignore, suppress or sacrifice any one of them, and look for that sweet spot when listening to your heart, mind and gut. There will be some trial and error, but when you find that sweet spot, you will know it, because that's the moment you say to yourself, 'Aha, this feels right!'

When these three elements work in alignment, your heart desires, your mind strategises, and your body actualises. You feel you are doing what you are put on the planet to do, you have a clearer life purpose and stronger personal relationships, and you have fewer physical health problems and an improved and overall healthier lifestyle. You feel 'right'.

STEP 3: EMBODY NEW PRACTICES

To upgrade your POS, you can integrate some practices into your everyday life that will heal and activate your vagus nerve, helping you to work with, instead of against, your body's natural rhythm. This will help you to maintain the balance of your autonomic nervous system and get access to endless renewable energy constantly and consistently.

The high levels of stress in modern life means that our sympathetic nervous system is constantly activated, while our parasympathetic nervous system is suppressed. When stress levels remain high for too long, the PNS can slowly lose its function. Stimulating the vagus nerve can 'wake up' the PNS. 'Vagal tone' is a clinical measure believed to indicate overall levels of vagal activity, and is measured indirectly through heart rate variability (HRV). A higher differential indicates high vagal tone.

You can improve vagal tone by choosing to incorporate one or all of these practices into your daily routine.

Practice 1: Breathe better

I remember the first day I met Angela. We have a mutual friend who suggested we have a chat, so we chose to meet in a local café on a bright Sunday morning.

She rushed in, quite apologetic for being less than one minute late. When she sat down, I noticed that her breaths were fast, short and shallow – the type of breathing you do when you're out of breath because you have been running super-fast or you are trying not to drown.

'Did you park far away?' I asked

'No, just across the road.'

'Sounds like you're out of breath. Did you run?'

'No, this is my normal way of breathing,' she said.

'How's your health?' I was curious.

'Not good. I cannot sleep well, and I was just recently diagnosed with a tumour in my stomach. It's benign, but quite big, and I also spent two weeks in hospital last year following a heart attack.'

'Is your life quite stressful?'

'I do have endless things to do, you know, when you have business and a family to support.'

'Are you the sole breadwinner for the family?'

'No, I'm not, my husband holds a senior role in corporate. All I need to do is to look after my children, and make good choices to grow our investment and monitor the business. I recruited people to run it after the heart attack.'

'Do you feel you have a lot on your mind?'

'Ah, yes, all the time.'

'Have you ever noticed the rhythm of your breath?'

'No, never. Anything wrong?'

Angela is a typical example of someone whose health is impaired by her way of breathing. Her short, shallow breaths constantly trigger the body's stress reaction. When the body is in stress reaction mode, less blood goes to the digestion and immune systems. If this continues, it can make you ill.

The first and most effective way to positively affect your vagus nerve is to learn to breathe correctly. Rapid, shallow chest breathing is a sign of stress, which activates the sympathetic branch of your ANS. Slow, deep, belly breathing is a sign of rest, which activates the vagus nerve and therefore the parasympathetic branch of the ANS.

There are many ways to relearn how to breathe properly. Here are some techniques you can explore.

Deep and slow belly breathing

Belly breathing, also called 'diaphragmatic breathing', allows more oxygen to come into your body.

When you breathe in deep and slowly through your nose and push down the diaphragm, there is more space for your lungs to expand and take in more oxygen. It also reduces the space that your heart can use, so your heart needs to pump out more blood, which in turn increases your heart rate and activates your SNS. When you take a long slow exhalation through your mouth, the diaphragm moves up and squeezes out more air from your lungs and leaves more space for your heart. This decreases your heart rate and activates your PNS.

Practising deep and slow belly breathing, say five to seven runs per minute, helps to activate the two arms of the ANS and bring them into balance.

Box breathing

Box breathing is a technique used to counter stress and anxiety. As suggested by its name, it means squared breathing, which can quickly bring your breathing pattern to a relaxed rhythm.

It goes like this:

- Take a slow deep breath for a count of four or six, until your lungs are full.
- Hold your breath for the same count (four or six).
- Slowly breathe out, for the same count, until your lungs are completely empty.
- Hold your breath for the same count.
- Repeat for thirty seconds or three minutes as needed.

Breathing and counting at the same time helps re-orient your attention and shift your focus away from the stressor that made you anxious. However, you don't have to be stressed to practise it; you can do it to reset and calm your mind and body any time you need to.

Heart coherent breathing

I know, I hear you: how can the heart breathe?

Heart coherent breathing is a technique developed by the HeartMath Institute, which involves breathing via your lungs but focusing your attention on your heart area, and it requires a bit of imagination. For example, when breathing in and out slowly through your nose, imagine you are doing so via your heart. It helps if you put your hands on your heart to centre your attention. Doing this for a few minutes helps to enhance the coherence between your mind and body, which leads to deep relaxation and clearer awareness.

In recent years apps have been developed to help us practise better breathing. **Calm** and **Breathwrk** are top rated apps that provide science-backed breathing exercises to regulate your stress level, improve mood, decrease fatigue and enhance performance.

Regardless of the method you use, the key is that through regular practise of these breathing techniques, you will enhance your ability to balance the two arms of the ANS, and be able to maintain a good breathing rhythm even when you feel stressed.

Practice 2: Eat better

As discussed already, your body is the engine for the other three operating systems. And if you want your body to behave like a superior machine, you need to feed it with superior fuel.

Eat to please your gut microbiome, not just your taste buds

As you already know, the food we eat changes the balance of microbes in our gut and our gut health has a direct impact on brain function.

So, what kind of foods are favoured by your gut?

Your gut loves fibre and diversity. For example, plant-based food, leafy green veggies, nuts and fruits, spices and green tea all promote the growth of good gut bacteria. Fermented food, such as yoghurt, kefir, kimchi and sauerkraut, are great sources of the probiotics that are needed by your gut.

While writing this book, the goal I set for my diet was to eat twenty-five to thirty different kinds of plant food per week, including nuts, veggies and spices. It may sound like a lot, but is quite doable.

Evidence suggests that excess red meat, especially processed meats, don't support our health, or gut health, especially when these products also contain antibiotics, hormones, pesticides and additives (in processed meats). Refined factory food full of sugar and additives, fried food, alcohol and excessive caffeine can all damage, or even kill, healthy gut bacteria.

In addition, sugar and alcohol both increase inflammation levels in your body, and also impair your brain function. For example, high blood glucose levels can cause the brain to atrophy or shrink, while alcohol interferes with the brain's communication pathways and can affect the way the brain looks and works. Over time, excessive drinking – like two or three glasses of wine a day – can increase your risk of potentially permanent brain damage. My bottom line is to avoid sugar and alcohol as much as I can. However, if consuming them provides you with a sense of joy and connection, well, go ahead and do it – just be aware of the price you are paying.

Your body is your engine, so fuel it smartly.

Use a phone app when shopping

When I started to care about the food I eat, it seemed like I had to double or even triple the time spent on grocery shopping. Reading labels requires a lot of patience. But there are tools out there that can help you.

For example, **FoodSwitch** is a free app available in many countries that allows you to scan the barcode of packaged foods using your smartphone camera. Using a traffic light labelling system, the app will tell you how healthy the food is based on its levels of unhealthy fat, sugar or salt.

Sugarfree is another free app that can be used to scan sugar content, track your daily water intake, and support you to build new lifestyle habits based on healthy eating.

Do a food sensitivity and intolerance test

In her book, *Feed Your Brain*, Dr Delia McCabe makes it clear that 'a *healthy brain starts with good nutrition ... because food influences hormones, neurochemicals and other key nutrients in the body. Any compound that irritates the brain or stops it from operating efficiently will eventually lead to neurobiological challenges.*[24]

If you're unknowingly eating foods that you're sensitive to or intolerant of, you may be exposing yourself to chronic inflammation. So do yourself a favour and invest in a food sensitivity and intolerance test. If you are in Australia, you can go to your GP or a qualified naturopath. Skin prick and specific IgE tests are covered by Medicare.

Practice 3: Move more in nature

Spending time in nature is excellent medicine for the madness of modern life.

There are studies that show that time spent in nature – as long as people feel safe – supports deeper reflection and assists stress management. It can lower blood pressure and stress hormone levels, reduce sympathetic nervous system arousal, enhance immune system function, reduce anxiety and improve mood.

Richard Louv, a journalist based in San Diego who wrote *Last Child in the Woods* in 2005, reviewed hundreds of studies on this subject and found that they all point in to one thing: *'Nature is not only nice to have, but it's a have-to-have for physical health and cognitive functioning.'*[25]

Japanese researchers have studied 'forest bathing' – a poetic term for walking in the woods. They found that people who practise forest bathing have optimum nervous system functions, well-balanced heart function and reduced incidence of bowel disorders.

There is also evidence showing that nature walks and other outdoor activities build attention and focus.[26] Strong environmental connections have been shown to be related to better performance, heightened concentration and reduced chances of developing attention deficit disorder.[27]

Add a dose of nature to your routine by walking your dog in the morning or hiking on the weekend, or simply by walking in a local park when you are having meetings online. Just a walk in the bush or a stroll on the beach on a sunny morning can awaken feelings of happiness and peace. Go bird watching, swim in the sea or just enjoy being in your garden and experiencing your connection to nature. It's good for the body and great for the soul.

Practice 4: Expose yourself to cold and heat

Have you heard of cryotherapy? This is an emerging science-based practice that is used to help reduce inflammation and activate healing via the parasympathetic nervous system. Cryotherapy involves deliberately exposing yourself to cold, and the simplest way to do this is by taking a daily cold shower.

If that sounds too hard, you can start by splashing your face with cold water. Then you can move on to immersing your forehead, eyes and at least two-thirds of both cheeks in cold water for thirty to sixty seconds. Slowly, you can also add a few seconds of cold exposure to the end of a warm shower, gradually building up to a full minute of cold.

Initially the cold will be shocking to your system and will change the way you breathe. Your goal is to take as many deep belly breaths as possible when your body is shivering from the cold. In this way, you are training your body to strengthen your vagus nerve and activate your PNS, which decreases heart rate, and turns on the immune system.

As the cold exposure becomes easier to bear – and it will – you can add a further one or two minutes of cold exposure per week until you shower entirely in ice-cold water and emerge with a huge smile on your face! A word of warning! Please don't do it at night, before sleep, though.

Deliberate exposure to heat is also good for you. How so?

Regular use of a sauna at a temperature between forty-five degrees Celsius and 100 degrees Celsius (depending on how hot it feels to you) and other heat exposure reduces mortality from cardiovascular events and stroke, and also reduces all-cause mortality.[28]

Heat exposure also decreases cortisol output, and if you take one sauna per week or every ten days, research suggests it increases growth hormone sixteen-fold.[29] Growth hormone impacts metabolism and the growth of cells and tissues in the body. It is responsible for tissue repair and growth spurts during puberty, but from the mid-thirties onwards growth hormone release is greatly diminished.

Practice 5: Rest to restore and renew

He that can take rest is greater than he that can take cities.

— BENJAMIN FRANKLIN

If you ask any physician, they will tell you rest is essential for health. If you ask any successful business leader, they will tell you that rest is essential for productivity.

For most leaders I have worked with, their idea of resting is binge watching videos, playing games, and spending time over-eating and over-drinking with family and friends. And I'm not saying you should not do these things – spending quality time with family and friends is actually quite important for us. What I am saying is that you should be smart about choosing the activities that can truly help you relax the body and restore and renew energy.

Research shows that binge watching Netflix or playing games may provide immediate gratification, but doesn't qualify as a good rest for the body. On the contrary, such activities can lead to sleeping problems, low self-esteem and low conscientiousness, and create depression and anxiety.[30] So if over-eating and over-drinking is your default way of socialising with the people around you, try to think of a better way!

Let's take a look at some different ways to rest and relax that are truly restorative.

Sensory rest

Do you feel tired all the time? Are you eating healthily and sleeping well and doing fine at work, but feel emotionally depleted? If so, it's time to take a sensory rest.

In her book *Sacred Rest*, Dr Saundra Dalton-Smith defines sensory rest as '*the opportunity to downgrade the endless onslaught of sensory input received from electronics, fragrances, and background noise.*' [31]

Bright lights, computer screens, background noise and multiple conversations can cause our senses to feel overwhelmed. Turning off all those sensory stimuli is the first step to rest and restore.

For example:

- If you spend a lot of time working with screens – computers, phones, laptops – then what might help you to rest and restore is a few hours away from screens. A walk in nature, a yoga session or a massage might balance your nervous system.

- If you spend a lot of time meeting and talking to people, a little solitary time might help you regain energy.
- If you spend a lot of time exhausting yourself by chasing goals and targets to stay on top of the game, then taking time to reconnect with your why, and re-experience that heart-felt vision you once had, might be useful to renew your energy.

Non-sleep deep rest (NSDR)

This is a term coined by Dr Andrew Huberman, a neurobiologist at the Stanford School of Medicine, to describe certain self-directed states of calm achieved through mental focus.

There are two specific NSDR protocols promoted by Dr Huberman: yoga nidra and self-guided hypnosis. Both enable you to get into a state of focus linked with relaxation.

Yoga nidra is a practice in which you lie down and listen to a guided meditation that helps you relax your body, bit by bit, and leaves you in a state of deep rest. As a popular practice, it can be accessed easily via YouTube or yoga apps. Down Dog is one of my favourite apps that allows me to practise all kinds of yoga anywhere, anytime.

Hypnosis as therapy is a very effective and safe treatment for many issues.

Dr. David Spiegle, the Medical Director of the Center for Integrative Medicine at Stanford School of Medicine, is a respected psychiatrist with over forty years' experience, and has studied hypnosis extensively. In his view, you can hypnotise yourself to achieve a state of focused attention, giving you greater control over your emotions and bodily sensations, and reduced self-consciousness. Dr Spiegle created a free self-hypnosis app called **Reveri**, which provides guided self-hypnosis exercises that take only eight to twelve minutes.

If you prefer a bit of high-tech for your NSDR, you might like to give **Muse** a try. Muse is a brain-sensing headband. Using a series of built-in sensors, it offers EEG-powered meditation and sleep support by measuring and analysing your level of brain activity, heart rate and breath simultaneously.

Muse was the very first biofeedback device I used, and it has been one of my favourites. In the past I found it a great tool to help me 'turn my brain off' and quickly send me into a meditative state. I must confess that I was a bit addicted to it for a while, and found the refreshing feeling after using Muse motivated me to use it every day. Rest is a skill, so polish yours!

Practice 5: Work with your rhythm
Your body includes your brain, and your body operates on rhythms! These rhythms function as 'internal clocks' that are in charge of our sleep patterns, mood, alertness, focus level, physical strength and energy level.

For business leaders, there are two important rhythms that require your attention:

Circadian rhythm
This is the rhythm that manages your mind, body and behaviours across a twenty-four-hour cycle. It responds to lightness and darkness in your environment, as well as your food intake, and is considered to be your body's 'master clock', working with other

bodily clocks to regulate your body temperature and hormone levels.

Research on mice shows that messing with the circadian rhythm results in early ageing and shorter lifespans.[32] In humans, obesity, cancer and cardiovascular diseases are quite common for those who have misaligned their circadian rhythm.[33]

When you work long hours and ignore your circadian system, the physiological processes that are designed to work during your awake time and slow down during sleep, such as digestion and immune system function, will be disrupted. This will lead not just to sleep loss, but difficulty waking in the morning, tiredness throughout the day, and even depression and stress.

Research published in 2018 showed that disrupting this sleep-awake pattern (in other words, sleeping during the day or working overnight) for as little as two nights altered 127 proteins that were 'associated with biological pathways involved in immune function, metabolism, and cancer', resulting in heart disease, depression, cancer and diabetes.[34]

Pulling an overnighter is not the only way to disrupt the circadian rhythm. Sleeping too little during the week (less than seven hours for adults) or sleeping several hours late on the weekend all count as disruptions to this body clock.

Modern-day workers also tend to stay inside longer and use artificial light day and night, but have limited exposure to sunlight. This can result in a feeling of 'jet lag', and it can be challenging to get up in the morning. Eating late or exercising late also alerts your body to stay awake and affects the function of this master clock.

Ultradian rhythm

This is another super important inner clock of the body. It runs on a shorter cycle, and it regulates the rhythm of blood circulation, heart rate, pulse and appetite, and repeats over a twenty-four-hour period.

As a business leader, your ultradian rhythm plays a huge role in your performance, particularly your mental performance.

When you start to focus on a task, it usually takes about sixty to ninety minutes to reach the apex of your productivity. After about 120 minutes, your performance or productivity starts to decline. You may notice that your body starts to get heavy, and your ability to focus and concentrate starts to drop. You get distracted easily and, depending on your body's condition, you may crave caffeine or foods that are high in fat or sugar to spike up your blood sugar.

If you grab lollies, cake and coffee to push through this slump, you will feel that you can refocus again as if you're climbing back to the apex of productivity. But you may notice that in the next ninety to 120 minutes or so, your body and mind are running on a much reduced capacity.

The longer we ignore our ultradian rhythms, the more damage we do to our bodies. We might develop stomach pain, digestive distress, mood imbalances or accumulate fat stores, especially around the belly. We might even experience hair loss or thinning. I experienced all these in my thirties, and now I see a lot of these things in driven, hard-working business leaders.

Working with your body's rhythms might sound complicated if you haven't paid much attention to them, but it can be as simple as making small changes in your daily routines.

Working with your rhythms means three basic things:

- Using bright, natural lights to wake your body up.

When getting up, ideally before 9 a.m., take yourself outside immediately and let the light get into your eyes. This triggers a chain of reactions in your physical body that sets the circadian rhythm, which means that when it gets darker, your body will start to secrete melatonin, the hormone that helps you fall asleep.

- Dimming the lights after sunset to help your body slip into sleep.

After sunset, make sure there is no bright artificial light in your environment. Instead, dim the lights to calm your system and allow the body to continue to release melatonin and help you fall asleep.

- Taking regular breaks during the day.

Take active rest every forty-five or ninety minutes from your first peak performance moment. Close your eyes, turn off the alerts, do a simple body scan or meditation for four to ten minutes, or use the NSDR techniques described earlier to help you to get some deep rest.

What's next?

Energy is a precious commodity these days. When you are running a business, your time and resources are limited, but demands and problems come from all directions. Don't let a low energy supply affect your business. When you upgrade your POS, chances are that you will gain access to endless renewed energy provided by your body – you will have your **vitality**!

It is quite okay for us to work in highly demanding, highly stress-ful jobs, and honestly, leading a purposeful life does come with high levels of stress. Learning how to prioritise your daily activities and put interventions in place to recover from the stress is the secret for sustained success.

When you start to prioritise the health of your physical body, even just embodying the practices described in this chapter at a minimal level, you will experience a sharper mind, reduced stress, and improved creativity and productivity.

Here is a simple self-assessment to understand the current state of your POS.

Self-assessment: Physical Operating System

The scale for each statement is 1–5.
1 = the statement does NOT resonate with me at all
5 = the statement describes exactly the way things are in my life

	1	2	3	4	5
1. I feel energetic and can get things done all the time.					
2. I always feel well rested and refreshed when I wake up.					
3. I recognise the indicators of stress in my body.					
4. I notice how different foods and drinks affect my thoughts, bodily sensations, moods and emotions.					
5. I relax and recharge my batteries regularly.					
6. I'm mindful of what I eat and drink.					
7. My lifestyle supports my wellbeing and makes me feel good.					

My score is: _____

You are the source of your superpowers

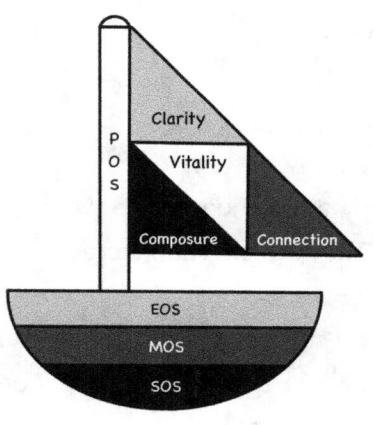

People do not decide their futures. They decide their habits and their habits decide their futures.

— F.M. ALEXANDER

Remember Leo, the obese perfectionist who ran a fast-growing PR company? When I met him in 2017 he was overweight and bad-tempered and had all his employees running scared. His business was in danger of closing down.

Meet him today.

Leo didn't close his business, and in fact his team is

growing. He committed to upgrading his internal operating system, including paying attention to his physical health and regulating both his diet and exercise. He has lost thirty kilos, he has married, and now has a newborn baby.

He told me, 'The moment I started to work on myself, everything started to transform. I put my energy, time and focus on myself – specifically on my thoughts, feelings and purpose. And when I did, not only did I feel better within myself, but everything around me began to change for the better.'

Your inner operating systems are the foundation for your performance, and ultimately influence the overall success you achieve in the long run. They are interconnected and intertwined. Each affects the others.

As soon as you start your self-upgrade, regardless of which operating system you begin with or the sequence in which you upgrade them, chances are high that you can start to get access to your superpowers.

These superpowers sit inside you. Sometimes they are hidden, and sometimes they require work from you to polish them up, but they are there. And they are the essence of who you are and enable you to leave your legacy to the world.

From the moment you start to work on upgrading your inner operating systems – not just after the upgrade is complete – you may notice that you begin to benefit from your hidden and not-yet-revealed superpowers. Those superpowers include **composure**, **connection**, **clarity** and **vitality**.

COMPOSURE

Being composed under stress is a leadership superpower.

As the leader of your business and your team, you need to show more composure than ever before in the workplace. How you respond to changes and other growing pressures is an indicator of your true fitness and ability as a leader.

Regardless of the tremendous credentials you may have, if you lack the ability to remain calm you will often make your employees feel uneasy. If you are unable to reinvent yourself and adapt to the unexpected, your tenure will be short-lived.

Being a composed leader, especially during times of uncertainty, adversity, crisis and change, means that you are constantly working on yourself to develop your leadership skills and professional maturity. You are actively trying to ensure that people feel safe and secure around you.

You will become a leader with composure when you upgrade your inner operating systems.

When your **EOS** is upgraded, you won't let your emotions get in the way.

You will find effective ways to process and utilise your emotions. If you do need to yell or get overly animated when times get tough, you will yell and get overly animated on purpose and in a safe way and place where your outburst will not damage your employees' faith in you. It will be your mindful choice, not your unconscious automatic reaction.

At the same time, by knowing your emotions intimately, you gain the power to use them to guide and motivate you and your team to fulfil your ambitions, rather than letting them control you.

When your **MOS** is upgraded, you won't jump to conclusions and take things personally.

You will build a hygiene bubble between you and the outside world so that you don't take issues to heart. This means you won't allow the noise and politics around you to suffocate your thinking and decision-making capabilities. In turn, you can maintain a positive mental attitude and manage a narrative that keeps you and the people you lead inspired and motivated.

When you believe that 'only the best things happen to me' and 'I will never be tested beyond my capacity', you will be fearless when facing the challenges and curve balls that come your way. You will know that these things are your opportunity to branch out of your comfort zone and outperform your limited self.

When you **SOS** is upgraded, you will be able to manage the fear imposed by your ego.

Remember that the ego's job is to protect you and to make you feel good about yourself. Fear is one of the tools it uses to stop you from stretching yourself and getting out of your comfort zone. However, when you see the connections between your inner world and your outer experience, you take challenges as a chance to insert your character, to align WHO you truly are with HOW you achieve.

When your **POS** is upgraded, you will be able to manage your impulses.

You know what might activate your stress reactions and what you can do to tame it. You can also control your desire for immediate gratification and therefore regulate your impulses. With this composure, you won't make impulsive poor choices that might harm yourself or others later. You also won't react poorly when you don't get what you want at the time you want it.

Being able to control yourself is a sign that you are a reliable leader that people can follow. You are an accountable leader who is fully committed to resolving the issue at hand.

CLARITY

'Clarity is the key to effective leadership,' as stated by Brian Tracy. It is the second leadership superpower you will have access to when your inner operating systems are upgraded and aligned.

It gives you a knowingness that is different from the analytical thinking you use when you're trying to figure something out.

We've all had an experience where we just know what to do, when our bodies give us a very clear message about what to do. It's as simple as knowing that we're hungry or thirsty. It's a feeling that you have to stay connected to. It's not in our conscious control. The knowingness and the clarity will produce thoughts, but thoughts that are different from the pinball thinking that we sometimes have, when our thoughts ping around and bounce off walls and refuse to stay still.

We are living in a world of noise, competition and information overload. We have an excessive amount of stimulation and information bombarding us from all angles, and it's easy to have a mind that is overloaded, cluttered, restless and chaotic. It's easy to get distracted. We quickly lose our direction, we make choices amid this chaos – where there is a lack of clarity – and end up somewhere we don't want to be. Then, we have to spend (waste) time trying to redirect our course.

Particularly in the middle of the chaos, playing your superpower of clarity makes a huge difference. Think of clarity as a verb – a way to seek an understanding of what makes sense, what to do, and where to go with your next step in life.

When your **SOS** and **EOS** are upgraded, you are clear about your purpose and vision. You love to ask 'Why?' This is how you discover your emotional drive for doing something you want to do. You also habitually ask 'What for?', which moves you towards a purpose that you hope to fulfil. A clearly defined purpose and vision make it easier for you to deal with complexity and make difficult decisions. They also keep you motivated, focused and organised through the process, and distractions become just noise for you.

A fit body and fit mind go hand in hand. When your **MOS** and **POS** are upgraded, stress won't harm your body. Instead, you will have endless energy to support your brain to work, and your ability to focus and to take multiple perspectives will be improved. You will think fast, quickly and, most importantly, deeply. Your vision will be far and wide, but you will also be able to notice what is near and now, and you will be able to make unclouded judgements. You will know exactly what value to add and what to offer without following the crowd and trapping yourself in the rat race.

When you know yourself, you will know how you operate and what causes a stall in your work or relationships. You will understand the value of simplifying your surroundings and quieting the noise in your head. You know what to listen to, what to hear, what to offer, what to stand for and what to communicate.

As a superpower, clarity gives you a clear vision, guilds you to walk in the right direction, allows you to plan and actualise your goals, and, most importantly, enables you to make sound and wise decisions amid chaos. You will grow your business in your unique way as who you are, not just as a copycat following the crowd.

CONNECTION

Connection is defined as a relationship in which a person or thing is linked or associated with something else. No matter how big or small your company is, connected leaders are thriving leaders who are not afraid to be vulnerable, who genuinely care about people, and who encourage collaboration and innovation.

Connected leaders are also able to connect the dots and see the relationships between self and the wider system. They can make sense of effort and outcomes, as well as motivations and behaviours.

Connection is a by-product of investing in upgrading your inner operating system.

When your **MOS** is upgraded, you will be able to hear yourself think, and be able to create mental space for deep thinking and enquiry. You will find the connections between your thinking-feeling-doing, and start to see your patterns, which are usually unconscious to you, but obvious to trained eyes.

When you work on upgrading your **POS** and **EOS**, you are enhancing the connection between your mind and body. When you practise breathing, you are also sharpening your present moment awareness. When you stretch your body, you are strengthening your mind to be more flexible. When you feed your body with premium 'fuel', you are taming the fires inside it and giving yourself a sense of control when you feel stressed or anxious.

When you work on upgrading your **SOS**, you ask yourself questions about the person you are, you look for deeper meaning in your life, you discover your deeply buried motivations and analyse recurring patterns. This helps you to see that you have control over your destiny, and that the chain of events that happened *to* you actually happened *for* you.

When your superpower of connection is activated, you find joy in exploring new things and advancing them more rapidly on your own. You don't necessarily approach things the same way. You can connect the dots in many aspects of your business and life – even dots that didn't seem to exist in the past.

As a business leader with such a superpower, you will be capable of seeing what is hidden, opening more doors, building more bridges, and forging and cultivating understanding, acceptance, inclusiveness, collaboration and even creativity in your business. Can you imagine what that would lead you to?

VITALITY

Vitality comes with a sense of liveliness. It allows you to approach life with excitement and energy; no longer will you do things half-heartedly – you are alive! You have inner resources that you created that produce abundant energy for you to use.

As business leaders, you need vitality to sustain your creativity, productivity and profitability. Your people look up to you for being both mentally and physically fit. Like a top-notch athlete, you manage yourself, your body and your mind as carefully as you manage your business. This allows you to deliver consistent and purposeful outcomes.

Upgrading your inner operating systems grants you access to the superpower of vitality.

When your **POS** is upgraded, you have the energy that allows you to do the work you want with endurance and flexibility. You will feel capable, energetic and healthy every day, which provides the life sources for all the other operating systems. You can use your body to handle whatever your life or business requires of you.

When our **EOS** is upgraded, we bring energy with us when we interact with self and others. Beyond just regulating our emotions, we harness the power of emotions, we are highly self-aware, and develop sound skills to work with our emotions. We won't let strong emotions control or blind us. Instead, we will be able to choose a positive, confident, cheerful, optimistic, hopeful and upbeat attitude that allows us to be at our best all the time.

An upgraded **MOS** provides the energy that keeps our minds sharp and focused, so that we can be alert yet relaxed, conscious yet flexible, focused yet open... When your **POS** can consistently provide a steady flow of oxygen-and-nutrients-rich blood to your brain, your perceptions will be clearer and you can think more sharply and effectively.

An upgraded **SOS** provides energy that allows us to be engaged and inspiring. When you lead a purposeful and meaningful life, you will experience endless joy and devotion. We won't let self-limiting thoughts or ego-driven fear hold us back. Instead, your actions and choices are motivated from within. While you might find life challenging from time to time, you will also experience a flow that fills you with joy, satisfaction and contentment.

As with other types of energy, vitality is not an endless resource. Energy depletion is the warning sign that you need to take time out to recover and renew – something that is usually neglected by high-achievers. But when your inner operating system is upgraded, you will understand the value of self-care and how it affects all aspects of your life and work.

You will be more sensitive to your energy level. You will learn to arrange your time and tasks according to your energy level and energy needs, which is the key to sustained high performance. It is not about how much time you have, but how much energy you have to do how much effectively.

As you consciously upgrade you inner operating system, you will produce your own renewable energy and become the source of your sustained success.

What's next?

~~~~~~~~~~~~~~

I hope the ideas and information I have presented in this book resonate with you. Perhaps you have recognised yourself in one of the leaders I discussed whom I have worked with. Most importantly, I hope that you have found a few practices to begin incorporating in your life as you work towards a full system upgrade. You don't have to change everything at once – start small and build from there.

'But where should I start?', you might be asking. Having an overview of where you are at in terms of the default settings of your inner operating systems might be a good place to start.

- You can take a self-assessment to see which of your operating systems are most in need of an upgrade, and start from there. Jump online here, www.ellazhang.com.au/book, to download the questionnaire.
- You can also participate in the online course and mastermind group coaching if you are keener, or
- If you are ready, reach out to discuss how you can optimise your company's people strategy in alignment with your upgraded inner operating systems.

Bon voyage!

About the Author

Ella Zhang is a passionate yet strategic workplace change maker, workshop facilitator and executive coach with decades of experience in Fortune 100 companies and start-ups. Her areas of expertise include leadership development, cultural transformation and talent development. Ella regularly writes about training and development, and has been a guest lecturer for EMBA students on topics like strategic HRM and leadership.

She holds Master's degrees in coaching psychology, commerce in business, and law. Ella leverages her expertise in adult education, spirituality, neuroscience and philosophy to assist individuals and businesses to reveal, expand and optimise their performance sustainably from the inside out. She is obsessed by the following questions at both an individual and organisational level:

- *Why do we do the things we do the way we do?*
- *How can we improve the way we do things?*
- *What can be different but better?*

Ella's seasoned business acumen and fine-tuned systems thinking skills enable her to support business leaders to master their inner games – the games within themselves and within their businesses – to actualise their deepest aspirations and achieve well beyond any worldly definition of success.

If you like, you can:

- connect with her on LinkedIn: linkedin.com/in/ellazhangsyd/, or
- write to her at ella@igrowingcapacity.com

Endnotes

1   Dr Carol S. Dweck, Mindset, Robinson, 2012, Chapter 1, Kindle

2   Janssen, CP, Gould, SJJ, Li, SYW, Brumby, DR, Cox, AL (2015). Integrating knowledge of multitasking and interruptions across different perspectives and research methods. International Journal of Human-Computer Studies, 79 pp. 1-5. 10.1016/j.ijhcs.2015.03.002.

3   Faria Sana, Tina Weston, Nicholas J. Cepeda, Laptop multitasking hinders classroom learning for both users and nearby peers, Computers & Education, Volume 62, 2013, Pages 24-31, ISSN 0360-1315,

https://doi.org/10.1016/j.compedu.2012.10.003. (https://www.sciencedirect.com/science/article/pii/S0360131512002254)

4   Watson, J.M., Strayer, D.L. Supertaskers: Profiles in extraordinary multitasking ability. Psychonomic Bulletin & Review 17, 479–485 (2010). https://doi.org/10.3758/PBR.17.4.479

5   Berman, M. G., Jonides, J., & Kaplan, S. (2008). The Cognitive Benefits of Interacting With Nature. Psychological Science, 19(12), 1207–1212. https://doi.org/10.1111/j.1467-9280.2008.02225.x

6   Mrazek, M. D., Franklin, M. S., Phillips, D. T., Baird, B., & Schooler, J. W. (2013). Mindfulness Training Improves Working Memory Capacity and GRE Performance While Reducing Mind Wandering. Psychological Science, 24(5), 776–781. https://doi.org/10.1177/0956797612459659

7   John J. Miller, Ken Fletcher, Jon Kabat-Zinn, Three-year follow-up and clinical implications of a mindfulness meditation-based stress reduction intervention in the treatment of anxiety disorders, General Hospital Psychiatry, Volume 17, Issue 3, 1995, Pages 192-200, ISSN 0163-8343, https://doi.org/10.1016/0163-8343(95)00025-M.

8   Kristen Neff, Self Compassion, the proven power of being kind to yourself, Kindle Ed., HarperCollins, 2011

9   https://dictionary.apa.org/emotion

10   Steffen, P. R., Hedges, D., & Matheson, R. (2022). The Brain Is Adaptive Not Triune: How the Brain Responds to Threat, Challenge, and Change. Frontiers in Psychiatry. https://doi.org/10.3389/fpsyt.2022.802606

11   Neria Y, DiGrande L, Adams BG. Posttraumatic stress disorder following the September 11, 2001, terrorist attacks: a review of the literature among highly exposed populations. Am Psychol. 2011 Sep;66(6):429-46. doi: 10.1037/a0024791. PMID: 21823772; PMCID: PMC3386850.

12   Mendes, Natalie, "How do emotions affect Productivity? [New research]", 29th Nov, 2017 https://www.atlassian.com/blog/software-teams/new-research-emotional-intelligence-in-the-workplace

13   Stein S, Book H. The EQ Edge: Emotional Intelligence and Your Success. 3rd ed. Jossey-Bass; 2011:17.

14   Breuning, Loretta Graziano. Habits of a Happy Brain. Kindle ed., Simon & Schuster, 2015

15   Breuning, Loretta Graziano. Habits of a Happy Brain. Kindle ed., Simon & Schuster, 2015

16   David, Susan, Emotional Agility. Kindle ed., Penguin, 2016

17   Taylor, Jill Bolte, My stroke of Insight. Kindle ed., Hodder & Stoughton, 2008

18   Mergenthaler P, Lindauer U, Dienel GA, Meisel A. Sugar for the brain: the role of glucose in physiological and pathological brain function. Trends Neurosci. 2013 Oct;36(10):587-97. doi: 10.1016/j.tins.2013.07.001. Epub 2013 Aug 20. PMID: 23968694; PMCID: PMC3900881.

19 Sara L Hargrave, Sabrina Jones, Terry L Davidson, The outward spiral: a vicious cycle model of obesity and cognitive dysfunction, Current Opinion in Behavioral Sciences, Volume 9, 2016, Pages 40-46, ISSN 2352-1546,

https://doi.org/10.1016/j.cobeha.2015.12.001.(https://www.sciencedirect.com/science/article/pii/S2352154615001801)

20 PERLMAN, R.M. (1954), THE AGING SYNDROME. Journal of the American Geriatrics Society, 2: 123-129. https://doi.org/10.1111/j.1532-5415.1954.tb00884.x

21 James A. Mortimer, Yaakov Stern, *Physical exercise and activity may be important in reducing dementia risk at any age,* Neurology Feb 2019, 92 (8) 362-363; DOI: 10.1212/WNL.0000000000006935

22 Hwang J, Castelli DM, Gonzalez-Lima F. The positive cognitive impact of aerobic fitness is associated with peripheral inflammatory and brain-derived neurotrophic biomarkers in young adults. Physiol Behav. 2017 Oct 1;179:75-89. doi: 10.1016/j.physbeh.2017.05.011. Epub 2017 May 10. PMID: 28501557.

23 Carabotti M, Scirocco A, Maselli MA, Severi C. The gut-brain axis: interactions between enteric microbiota, central and enteric nervous systems. Ann Gastroenterol. 2015 Apr-Jun;28(2):203-209. PMID: 25830558; PMCID: PMC4367209.

24 McCabe, Delia, Feed Your Brain. Kindle ed., Exisle, 2016

25 White, M.P., Alcock, I., Grellier, J. et al. Spending at least 120minutes a week in nature is associated with good health and wellbeing. Sci Rep 9, 7730 (2019). https://doi.org/10.1038/s41598-019-44097-3

26 Hartig, T., Mang, M., & Evans, G. W. (1991). Restorative effects of natural environment experiences. Environment and Behavior, 23(1), 3-26.

27 Faber Taylor, A., & Kuo, F. E. (2009). Children with attention deficits concentrate better after walk in the park. Journal of Attention Disorders, 12(5), 402-409.

28 Rhonda P. Patrick, Teresa L. Johnson, Sauna use as a lifestyle practice to extend healthspan, Experimental Gerontology, Volume 154, 2021, 111509, ISSN 0531-5565, https://doi.org/10.1016/j.exger.2021.111509.

29 Rhonda P. Patrick, Teresa L. Johnson, Sauna use as a lifestyle practice to extend healthspan, Experimental Gerontology, Volume 154, 2021, 111509, ISSN 0531-5565, https://doi.org/10.1016/j.exger.2021.111509.

30 Starosta JA, Izydorczyk B. Understanding the Phenomenon of Binge-Watching-A Systematic Review. Int J Environ Res Public Health. 2020 Jun 22;17(12):4469. doi: 10.3390/ijerph17124469. PMID: 32580289; PMCID: PMC7344932.

31 Dalton-Smith, Saundra. Sacred Rest. Kindle ed., Hachette Book Group, 2017

32 Roman V. K, Anna A. K, Victoria Y. G, Olena V. V, and Marian P. A, Early aging and age-related pathologies in mice deficient in BMAL1, the core componentof the circadian clock. Genes & Dev. 2006. 20: 1868-1873. doi:10.1101/gad.1432206

33 Broussard JL, Van Cauter E. Disturbances of sleep and circadian rhythms: novel risk factors for obesity. Curr Opin Endocrinol Diabetes Obes. 2016 Oct;23(5):353-9. doi: 10.1097/MED.0000000000000276. PMID: 27584008; PMCID: PMC5070789.

34 Depner, Christopher M, Melanson, Edward L, McHill, Andrew W, Wright, Kenneth P, Mistimed food intake and sleep alters 24-hour time-of-day patterns of the human plasma proteome, 2018, Proceedings of the National Academy of Sciences, E5390-E5399, 115.23, doi:10.1073/pnas.1714813115, https://www.pnas.org/doi/abs/10.1073/pnas.1714813115

www.ingramcontent.com/pod-product-compliance
Lightning Source LLC
Chambersburg PA
CBHW061146120626
46546CB00005B/1956